The Empire of the Heart

The Empire of the Heart

John Harriott

Templegate Publishers
Springfield, Illinois

Gracewing.

Leominster, Herefordshire
England

Copyright © 1990 John Harriott

First published in the United States of America by
Templegate Publishers
302 East Adams Street
P.O. Box 5152
Springfield, Illinois 62705
ISBN (USA) 0 87243 175 4

First published in the United Kingdom by
Gracewing / Fowler Wright Books Ltd.
Southern Avenue, Leominster
Herefordshire HR6 OQF England
ISBN (UK) 0 85244 192 4

CONTENTS

FOREWORD

It was one of the blessings of an old-fashioned Catholic education that one grew up with the bemused impression that all popes were bad except the current incumbent. With commendable objectivity many of my own teachers seemed determined, while giving full value to the graces that flow to us through membership of the Church, to inoculate their charges against the presumption that life within it is all sweetness and light. Alongside the Church's scriptures, sacraments and saints, and all its practical prescriptions for leading a devout life, they exposed with candour its sinfulness and corruption, the popes and prelates entrusted with its government and administration. Even if occasionally and misleadingly they seemed to imply that the hard times were over and we ourselves would not experience the same tensions as our forefathers—the saints, scholars and pastors who battled for internal reform, or the martyrs who went to the block knowing full well that Rome was a by-word for corruption, I am grateful to them. They pinpointed a problem in the experience of being a Catholic which is not a recent development but dates back to the earliest days of the Church, and is not occasional but almost a permanent feature of Christian life.

Catholics in earlier ages have had to reconcile their faith with private ownership of the papacy, presumptuous Roman claims to secular authority, official persecution of heretics, the lechery and luxury of Renaissance popes, catastrophic political alliances, the intellectual and doctrinal degeneration represented by the Syllabus of Errors, and much else. Today brings its own variant on this old theme; government by a kind of anticonciliar curial Broederbond bent on disenfranchising most of the national hierarchies as well as the ordinary clergy and laity.

Scandal in high places should not be glossed over or privately indulged, not only because it is an evil in itself but because as Pope John XXIII recognised, it obscures the genuine riches the Church has to offer and deters prospective believers who would benefit

7

from them. From the inside however, most of us know that we are no strangers to the temptations that beset the exalted, and that the chief obstacle to effective grace in our own lives is not their sins but our own.

That is to state the negative ground of the argument. The positive side is the experience and expression of living in a communion of faith existing now, reaching back into the past and forward into eternity, a communion where at every level and in everyday experience holiness and vision, learning and wisdom, self-sacrificing charity and passion for justice, humble service and quiet integrity are regularly encountered, and over the years steadily inspire, stimulate and reproach. Part of that experience is a sense of companionship with those universally recognised as holy, those who most clearly embody Christian ideals. At a more mundane level it includes a lifetime's encounter with men and women who will never be official saints but whose examples and influence have discovered to each of us facets of Christian faith and practice with compelling attraction. It is that experience which provides the very criteria by which institutional offences are recognised as such; which makes those offences endurable; and which makes it true to say that what really matters in Catholic life can only be adequately judged from the inside.

Again, the core of this communion and the key to its meaning and purpose is not a human administrative apparatus, good, bad or indifferent. It is the Eucharist. There the community of faith is made present and visible, expresses and articulates itself, finds its compass, is most profoundly instructed. That is the essential bond of faith, and here too continual immersion in the experience of it is the only way to grasp its full significance. Among much else it builds bridges across gulfs of culture, race, colour, custom and outlook which are beyond mere human engineering. Years ago I remember standing in a jungle clearing among hundreds of abjectly poor peasants at a Mass celebrated in Tagalog. In most respects their experience of life and mine were beyond mutual comprehension. Yet in and through that Mass we were of one mind and heart, we were all at home. And indeed wherever in the world Mass is celebrated, that is home. Human failings are always easily explicable. That kind of miracle is not. And for its sake one can learn to put up with much other discomfort.

8

'Without stirring abroad one can know the whole world; without looking out of the window one can see the way of heaven.' It seems a far cry from the Tao Te Ching to eighteenth-century rural England. But after reading the *Diary of a Farmer's Wife,* I'm not so sure. Its author was Anne Hughes, a young woman in her mid-twenties. She kept her diary from February 1796 to August 1797, often rising at night while her husband, John, who might think it female folly, was asleep. John Hughes was a prosperous, no-nonsense Herefordshire farmer, shrewd, practical, dearly loved, but short-fused and difficult to handle. Anne is up to the task. "I doe saye I thynke I will give Sarah (her servant) another 2 pense a weke wagges she bein steddie, and worken harde ande noe trouble toe us, atte wych hee didde laffe and call mee hussie butt agreede wyche didde please mee, but I dide not tell hym I hadde been doinge itt for a munthe nowe."

Anne records in fine detail the chores, visits, entertainments, burials, weddings, alarums and excursions of her village life. She and her little court of women—her idolised mother-in-law, her maid, Sarah, and the carter's wife who helps out—are kept hard at it tending the pigs and hens, copying out elaborate recipes, and cooking hams, 'hayres,' chynes of bacon, rounds of beef, roast chickens and rabbits for the gargantuan meals which relieved the daily grind. She is constantly breaking out her primmy rose or pansy wine, or home-made cider, for the visitors who call, or calming down her husband with a jorum of hot punch or the violet pudden "which is a good cure for cross husbands."

Animals sicken and have to be dosed. She fights a daily battle with the mud, snow and grease spots that invade her spotless kitchen floor. The deaths of friends and neighbours keep the funeral bell tolling and reduce her frequently to tears. The poor need aid and comfort. A ghostly light in a deserted cottage turns out to be a gypsy and his wife who have taken refuge. They are taken under her wing, at first without her husband's knowing, until she can persuade him that it is his idea to help them. So too is her neighbour's daughter who has an illegitimate child, and a poor woman who is sick and has a feckless husband, and the 'foggers' (casual labourers), and their 'trollopes' who help with the hay harvest. She reflects often that she herself has never known hunger, and how God has blessed her with "a goode husbun albeit a babbie att times, a goode home, ande above all, a deere mother I can love and honner allus."

Her world is a small one. A journey of twenty miles is an epic voyage, carefully prepared for. "I shall nott rite in mye littel book till I bee backe whyche I feer maye bee nevver when I doe thynke off thee miles I be goen toe travill. John's mother didd saye toe mee toe hide mye monies carefully for fear wee bee stopt, soe I hav putt almoste all in a bagge of chaffe, nigh 10 guineas in thee littel waine marked wythe a redd stringe toe knowe whyche one." They *are* stopt, and the carter's wife "who has a goode arme for hitten" presents a pistol at his head, but it is no highwayman, only a man asking the way. Even at home life has its dramas. Thieves break in and are roundly thrashed by the womenfolk. A cow is stolen, a sheep killed by lightning.

Anne never refers to war, politics or economics. Three years before her diary opens Louis XVI was executed and the Reign of Terror began; the year before, Warren Hastings was acquitted; while she is writing, Napoleon enters Milan, Jervis beats the Spanish fleet at Cape St Vincent, there is mutiny at the Nore, and Jenner introduces vaccination. She mentions none of them. These things are 'out there.' Her concerns are cleanliness, kindliness, and keeping her husband sweet. She is competent, practical, and highly skilled in her country crafts. She is thrifty, but generous to a fault, and thinks carefully of gifts and presents that will please. She has a genius for friendship, is grateful for her home, her comforts, the love and affection she receives. She treats her servant as an equal, and is hard on a farmer who uses his men as if they were but tools. She looks for the good in everyone but shrewdly sizes up those who are prim, snobbish, greedy or shiftless. She would have made a good Angel of the Last Judgment. And out of her tiny world she writes a book that is a delight to read two centuries later.

While the pound falls, the politicians bombinate, Beirut burns, and crazed ideologues tear at each other's throats, I like to think of her and the thousands like her who keep the wheels of the world turning. They have no grand theories, wish harm to no man, do not tinker with frontiers or force their ideas on those unwilling to accept them. They make shift to put food on the table, keep out the cold, do battle with dirt and decay, above all work hard at the difficult business of loving. England is very rich in them.

Anne Hughes may never have heard of Napoleon. But she built her empire in the heart, and perhaps it is more enduring. Frontiers may change, but the vital values and tasks of life are changeless. In her 'littel booke' she describes a sermon, one which unusually did not put her to sleep. "It didd please mee muche, for hee did nott tell us that thee divvel woulde hav us for caringe for our monies but didd saye thee worlde bee a verrie goode plase toe live in, and us toe live kindlie wythe our naybours, ande bee goode toe thee poore was thee true religgun, toe wyche I doe hartilie agree.'' Amen to that.

LESSONS FROM LUTHER

Listening recently to a radio programme about Martin Luther, I was much struck by the simplicity, even innocence, of the man, at least in his early days. Corruption in the Church is staring him in the face, contradicting the plain sense of the gospels, scandalising the faithful. So too is cynicism where should be ardent belief. Both are blatant, incontrovertible. Rome, the Pope, cannot be aware of what is going on. If he can only get a hearing, if only he can sit down quietly with the Pope's representatives, perhaps even the Pope himself, they will understand each other, they will see the same shining meaning in the gospels, they will understand him and realise how falsely his critics accuse him. Thank you, they will say, for pointing out these errors. Thank you for letting us know what is going on. Of course, something must be done.

And then the shock when he does meet papal representatives. Far from sitting down quietly as fellow-inquirers after truth, they will not even read the gospels and the fathers which are his evidence and witnesses; they will not read what he has written; they simply pick up words, phrases, out of context, from which they can make the case that he is a Hussite, a heretic. He tries to discover what concessions will win them over, what statements will give him a fair hearing. All they want is recantation, silence. Gradually the confidence oozes away, the trust is broken, the respect is withdrawn, and bitterness begins to set in. Painfully he discovers that their priorities are not as he imagined, that their goals are far different, that they are playing a different game. The suspicious, stubborn peasant in him takes over, and he accepts that he is on his own, his only guide the truth that is in him. We are still living with the results, 500 years later.

Now, I am no Luther scholar and cannot vouch for the truth of this account, though it seemed to be solidly based on his own writings, letters and transcripts of critical meetings and debates in which he had taken part. But it is certainly a paradigm of dealings between authorities, both secular and ecclesiastical, and awkward customers who make life difficult for them, right down to our own day. That tone of innocent confidence rings in so many protesting voices as they address those whom their anxieties apparently should

11

concern. At a humble level the old lady trying to get action from the gas or water board: villagers protesting against the blitzing of the countryside by local farmers; townspeople anxious to save their towns from disembowelling by planners. And back comes the bureaucratic voice with its standard reply: "We have taken your views into account and given them serious consideration but . . . But, you can't see the whole picture, we must preserve a balance of interests, we are doing everything possible in the circumstances. We must look to the long-term, go away and stop bothering us."

At the international level it is the voice of Solidarity addressing the Russians: "You say you're the champion of the working class, power to the people, the defender of workers' rights. Well, we're workers, we want a revolution, we have no power and no rights, listen to us, hear our case." It is the voice of the Nicaraguans addressing the Americans: "You say you're the champions of democracy, national self-determination, human rights. Well, we've just had the most popular revolution since your own, we just want to run our own country, we're trying to given everyone a fair deal and we have the whole people behind us. What more do you want, how do we prove our good faith? And back comes the standard superpower reply: "We must consider your request in terms of our own national interest; workers' rights, democracy, national, self-determination are phrases for the speech-writers — the realities are zones of influence, profits, national security. Grow up and try to understand the real world."

Cynical? Not so very. That pattern of confident appeal for a fair hearing to those with the power to change matters of a lack of sympathy where sympathy had been expected, of increasing disillusion with once respected authorities, is an everyday occurrence. And so too is its consequence. Once Luther had decided he must go it alone, was thrown back on his own powerful emotions, he had no check on ideas which became more extravagant and extreme. The chances of finding some common ground based on agreed truths were entirely lost. Luther's honest outrage became destructive. And the unity of Christendom, the papacy's proper and legitimate concern, was damaged on a scale which could scarcely have been foreseen. For want of a shoe the war was lost. It is a horrid warning for any authority whose actions belie its professed concerns, which tries to brush away honest grievances, and which thinks it can impose by brute force a solution which in fact can be achieved only by sympathetic understanding and dispassionate regard for truth. Perhaps a picture of Luther should be on every office wall.

HOW NOT TO USE AUTHORITY

What puts people off the Catholic Church? In one word, its authoritarianism. Not, note, its authority, rather its style of exercising authority. Recently I have been surprised how often this issue has cropped up in a variety of conversations with both members of other Christian denominations, including church leaders, and with people professing no religious beliefs whatever. At least in what is loosely called the Anglo-Saxon world, the image of Rome as an enemy to intellect and to personal conscience is deeply ingrained in the collective psyche, and still repels many people who find much else admirable and attractive in the Church's life and teaching. The figure of Giant Pope may have lost his original lurid paint-work but still, grey and weatherbeaten, he has power to affright Christians and non-Christians alike. For other Christians, that authoritarianism bars the way to Christian unity; for non-believers, it deters even the attempt to examine the Church's credentials and claims.

This strength of feeling has surprised me because the people concerned were by no stretch of the imagination ignorant or unsophisticated, either about the course of human history or about the nature of institutions. Yet all the following remarks have been made.

The Church is a mirror image of the Communist Party in its mode of dealing with dissent, and indeed the Party learned many of its techniques from church practice. The Church has no objective interest in the pursuit of truth but is primarily concerned to impose conformity with official, that is Roman, policy. The Church always prefers institutional interest to the good of individuals. The Church applies absolutist solutions to personal problems without regard to particular circumstances. Church discipline is exercised on both clergy and laity alike in a harsh and insensitive way. Catholics are more easily attracted than Protestants to totalitarian political ideologies, because Catholics cannot conceive of any form of social order which is not essentially authoritarian.

Now I, faced with these damaging charges, gobbled like a turkeycock, and so, no doubt, will most Catholic readers. Living inside the Church is a complex experience, and the reality of Catholic life is a good deal removed from what it may seem to the outsider. Even so, one could not protest with hand on heart that such charges contained no element of truth whatever, or that no events and incidents could be adduced in evidence to suport them. The billowing clouds of smoke may suggest a huge conflagration where there is actually only a small fire, but fire there surely is.

Whether the fire be large or small, the fathers at Vatican II seemed determined to put it out. And they were undoubtedly influenced by episodes of which they were all conscious when ideas had been condemned only later to be recognized as entirely compatible with Christian faith, or individuals had been harshly disciplined only later to be honoured by the whole Church for their probity and prophetic vision.

How to deal with differences in the Church is a problem which meets with no easy solution. The Church has authority to teach, must know its own mind, and must be able to express it. And there is a need for some degree of church order if the whole community is not to dissolve into warring sects. On the other hand, in any particular instance, it is important that it should be the mind of the universal Church which is genuinely being expressed, not that of some particular cultural faction; and that unfamiliar movements or ideas are not being ruled out simply on the grounds that they are unfamiliar. In practice, clarity may come only after a long exercise of patience, sustained dialogue, meditative reflection; and in the meantime there will be much uncertainty, much untidiness.

For some temperaments, that is too much to bear. They want decisiveness, order, almost at any cost. And the temptation then is to shift the issue from the arena of dialogue to the field of church discipline. The meeting of minds is reduced to a clash of wills. In the short term, this may bring quick results, an outward appearance of order. But if the issue is of any real importance, it will smoulder away subterraneously and break out again in other places and at other times and as like as not in a fiercer form. The supposedly decisive act turns out not to be the end of the matter but merely a holding action.

Whether in politics or religious matters, settling differences of opinion simply by bringing more guns to bear rarely if ever enhances authority or achieves a lasting peace. The lesson repeatedly asserts itself in other walks of life. The doubts and uncertainties grumble on. The humiliated are less, not more, likely to be convinced. That, I suspect, is what the council fathers were driving at: that authoritariansim is the enemy of authority, and that quashing dissent by main force may win battles but loses wars. And what they believed then still holds good now.

PROOF OF IDENTITY

A classic story is told of a young mother out walking her baby when a friendly stranger stopped her, peered into the pram and exclaimed, "What a beautiful child." "Oh," said the mother, apparently not much flattered, "you ought to see his photograph." The story is a favourite among media people—perhaps they should be called "mediacrities"—who are constantly fascinated by the inclination of television viewers and newspaper readers to regard the image as more real than the reality. Like the Northern Irish family who jibbed at being televised because they felt they were so colourless compared with the fictional families on the box.

As so often happens life is catching up with fiction. In these days of high security it becomes increasingly difficult to prove that one is who one thinks one is. Doubts begin to set in as, in all kinds of circumstances, bevies of petty officials ignore the flesh and blood before them and demand proof of identity. Only the Almighty is allowed to get away with the sublime and simple assertion, "I am who I am." The rest of us are not so lucky. Cheque books are waived aside as if they were out-of-date cigarette coupons. Bankers' cards need bankers' cards upon their back to prove 'em. Soon we will need two witnesses and a bible oath to buy a shirt at Marks & Sparks. The shortest shopping expedition becomes an obstacle race through checkpoints, and an airflight leaves a loungeful of passengers suffering crises of identity. Am I really me if everyone I meet seems to doubt it?

Not long ago a mechanic was mending his car in Nothern Ireland when he found he was missing some minor part. He got into the car to drive to the garage, and only when he came to an army checkpoint did it dawn on him that he had no identity card in the dungarees he was wearing. Thinking he might get away with it he drove up and confessed his omission to an attendant soldier. "Well," said the soldier, sympathetically, "have you a driving license?" "No," said the mechanic. "Or your insurance?" "No," the mechanic replied. "Well, have you anything to prove identity?" the soldier asked, trying to be as helpful as possible. The mechanic went through his pockets, looked frantically round the car, and came suddenly to rest as his eye caught the driving mirror. "Ah," he cried in triumph, "that's me all right."

Unlike your ordinary citizen, who has never felt the need to prove himself, priests have a long history of coping with what our Prime Minister has the trick of calling "these matters." Suspicious Mother Church has never considered an innocent countenance and a clean clerical collar as proof of authenticity. Before allowing priest-strangers to minister at her altars she likes to see accreditation from their bishop, an episcopal assurance that they are the real McCoy, or Murphy, or McCormack, as the case may be. And in these days when the skier sharing your snowdrift may turn out to be the Pope, or the jogger in the park your very own Archbishop, who's to say she's wrong?

But clerical guile or clerical simplicity can always find a way. There was, for example, the Indian priest who called into St Peter's to say Mass. He was somewhat nonplussed, when he arrived at the sacristy door, to spot a muscular monsignor checking the *celebret,* or license to celebrate. Having no such article about his person he was about to withdraw, when instinct whispered to him that the monsignor, though a brother in the Lord, might not belong to the great band of brothers who speak English. So boldly stepping forward, he flourished his driving licence, and to his great delight was nodded through.

A somewhat different case was that of my late priest uncle. One year, after a busy and exhausting Christmas, he decided he needed a break. It was in the days when his diocese was ruled by a bishop who did not recognise the need for breaks, either for himself or his parish priests. There was nothing for it but to take French leave. So, though by nature a dutiful man, early one morning my uncle crept down on clerical printless toe to Newcastle railway station and hied him to the Isle of Wight. There he stayed with friends, and the following day went over to the local Benedictine parish to celebrate Mass. To his horror, for he had long ago used it to light a cigarette, he was asked for his *celebret.* He implored, he expostulated, he turned out his pockets, he pointed to the green gloss of his suit and the crinkles in his shoes as evidence that he was the genuine article, but all to no avail. A bogus priest was at large in the diocese, the Benedictine told him, and the bishop had issued strict orders not to let strange clergymen so much as begin to vest. My uncle argued, but the Benedictine was adamant until, of a sudden, an idea struck him. "Why," he asked, "don't you ring your bishop and get him to vouch for you?" "Good heavens, man," my uncle exploded, "I don't even want him to know I'm out of the diocese." The Benedictine relaxed, patted him on the shoulder, and said, "That's all right, Father, you say Mass. I'll serve you myself." He knew the real thing when he met it.

AN ANCIENT FAMILY

Built into the jamb of the priest's door in the twelfth-century church at Sparsholt is a curious stone. On it are marked the lines and holes of six men's morris, a favourite game before and during the Middle Ages. The workmen, one presumes, who built the church, marked the stone to play on in their idle moments, and then, perhaps inadvertently, built it into the doorjamb where it remains to this day.

It is powerfully evocative. Who were the men who sat playing on that stone and scratched those marks? What did they look like, wear, talk about? Whose hand chiselled the marks? And could he ever have conceived that they would catch the interest and stir the imagination of people living in such a different age as ours, nine centuries later?

Traces of the past are part of our present. And nowhere more so than in an ancient house where the same family have lived for many generations. The very walls speak of enduring needs, skills and feelings which ancestors shared, and a hundred human traces bring them alive. Here a wing has been demolished and there another thrown up. Here changes of taste have hidden ancient timbers behind a new facade, and there mutations in social habits have closed up windows and doorways and remodelled rooms. On every side lie evidences of the family's fortunes, affections, outlook and activities: portraits, pictures, books and instruments, keepsakes, weapons and utensils, surviving from different ages; stains and marks and worn stones that human hustle and bustle have left as records of old accidents and routine. And there are stories and associations for handing on, of a room, a person, an object; wisps of memory, fragments of legend, capsules of family lore keeping a sense of continuity alive no less than documents and letters handed down. Even on the visitor such centres of tradition cast a powerful spell. For those born into such a house, the past must shape their whole outlook on the present.

The Church is such a house and such a family. The Christian lives in two dimensions, the present and the past. From the hour of his baptism he enters an old house and an ancient family, inheriting its wisdom and treasures, its keepsakes, its memories, its lore. He too looks back to generations of ancestors who speak across the centuries, to moments of glory and times of misfortune, to the traces of a continuing vibrant daily life. He, too, finds himself inheriting an outlook, a store of family associations and experience, heroes and significant events. He is not born into a howling wilderness with neither stars to steer by nor signposts to point his way. He is not pitched into darkness, nor thrown back solely on his own resources, nor asked to struggle from scratch with the bewildering mysteries of life and death. He finds himself caught up in a living tradition where both change and continuity have their place, embraced by a family which offers him resources, companionship, the lessons of experience, a birthright, a sense of direction. And in this instance the family he joins reaches, both in the past and in the future, beyond the grave.

17

This, it seems to me, is part of the answer to those who wish to lead a Christian life without the Christian institution. Of course, like family tradition, the Christian institution can lay on burdens as well as offer enrichment. Like an ancient family, the Church has a chequered past and suffers present discords. Irritation, resentment, disappointment, even scandalised feelings, are the price of belonging to any community vulnerable to human failings and defects. Like an ancient family the Church also has its skeletons in the cupboard, its rogues and black sheep, its fools and incompetents, as well as its saints and heroes and wise men. It too has known periods of decline as well as times of prosperity.

Yet surely this weighs little against the riches that attach to family membership. Outside the house, the lone individual is shut within the circle of his own personal experience. Inside the house, no matter the draughts and leaks and family quarrels, his mind is enlarged and fed, his affections warmed, his imagination stimulated in a thousand ways. The inherited family wisdom at least gives him a frame of reference for his own wrestling with the meaning of existence, a wisdom that has been gathered through many centuries and from many cultures. So many great figures from the past turn out to be his kinsmen. So many among the world of strangers he has entered prove to have family ties. So many places, objects, antiquities which otherwise he might have looked on with cold curiosity take on a personal meaning for him. And there is ceremony to order, interpret and solemnise the events and stages of his mortal existence. To be inside this house is to be enlarged and enriched socially, morally, culturally and spiritually.

At least that is how it should be, at least that experience is possible. The problem is to make it a living reality, not just for a happy few, but for all.

NICKY'S WORLD

Nicky is eleven and enjoying Christmas already, several weeks ahead. His mysterious early warning system signals birthdays, highdays and holidays well in advance, and he moves towards them in slow motion rapture. Unless miracles happen he will never read, write, vote, marry, have a home of his own, never travel alone, and positively never be a useful member of society: but he has his secrets. He requires constant care, watching, stimulation, which he receives in abundance from his family and an 'aunt', now in her eighties, who shares with him a private world of mutual devotion which few of us, perhaps, can ever plumb.

Nicky, you may have gathered, is mentally handicapped, a Down's syndrome child, not a desperate case but bad enough. I first saw him when he was one year old, crouched on the kitchen floor, his face smattered with tears, like a ruined goblin. Within four days of his birth he had a colostomy, which a year later was closed up. He has had plenty of pain since, and been frequently in and out of hospital. Now he is a chunky, tough youngster, always on the go. When still, he stands stiff-legged with his toes turned in, his head at an angle, his arms jerking in a kind of 'Kamerad' gesture, his eyes swallowing everything going on around him, his face creased in a huge ragged-toothed grin. He chortles and gurgles his way through life. His smile draws answering smiles out of the tired, the worried and the downcast. On a recent walk along a narrow river towpath he greeted every pensive stranger out for a Sunday stroll with a roaring whoop and a massive hug: they all went on their way plainly delighted by an experience all too rare.

Nicky is an innocent Falstaff, not only mirthful in himself but the cause of mirth in others. 'What a life! What a life!' he sighs, mimicking his aunt; 'It really is a life with you!' Or, floundering into the sitting-room in an elder brother's waterproofs, 'All right, I'll be off now'. To Nicky the local priest is Father God. One of the sisters at the local convent which often mothered him and gave him splendid teas (at which he insisted they read 'Jesus books') became Sister Jelly. He finally rewarded the sisters by spraying them all with scent. Lourdes he associates with his favourite form of conveyance, an elevator. The highpoint of Sunday Mass is the Kiss of Peace, when he goes round the church gleefully hugging everyone in sight. He has manic enthusiasms, for ball games or fireworks, or, more piously, reciting the Our Father crouched under the piano.

There is nothing purely angelic about Nicky. He can be moody, cantankerous, angry. His sentences swell and fade like an old wireless set, articulate speech interspersed with bouts of rhetorical blather. He has a sly eye for mischief, a taste for leg-pulling. If his parents are going out to dinner he will slip away, dressed in his best clothes and come downstairs with loud, imperious cries of 'Let's go!' Asked what he has been doing at school he answers tersely, 'Mince, potatoes and custard'.

Not so long ago his mother took him out on the local common. Nicky's idea of a walk is a series of retriever-like explorations of the undergrowth. On this occasion his mother kept him moving smartly forward while pointing out interesting flora and fauna. He trailed along mutinously, muttering to himself. Suddenly she caught the words. 'Bloody mud' he was saying, 'Bloody donkeys, bloody trees, bloody squirrels'. And finally, with thunderous inconsequence, 'Bloody rice-pudding'.

Well in the running for the nation's No. 1 television viewer, Nicky has long been established as Keeper of the Family Set. The only programme he will not watch is the News, and he has invented countless dodges to get it switched off. He must, however, be the only person in the land who sits entranced through all the political party annual conferences: left, right, dead centre, they have him on the hook. Just as he can distinguish gramaphone records despite his total inability to read, so he has no difficulty in rattling off the day's forthcoming programmes with perfect accuracy. He knows, too, all the faces of the presenters and performers. 'Ah', he will say, poking his head round the door, 'Alithtair Cooke' or 'Benny Hill'. His taste is catholic. One day his mother came in while he was watching a football match, and turning down the sound sat at the far end of the room to listen to some music. Nicky at once came over and said firmly, 'Use earphones'. 'No', she said, 'I'm listening to the music. You don't need the sound'. 'I can't hear' he insisted. 'What can't you hear?' she asked. 'I can't hear the dithcushion'. The idea of Nicky absorbed by soccer pundits discoursing on Laying it Off and Running into Space, reduced everyone to paroxysms.

It is easy, of course, to romanticise the handicapped. Their pain and frustration are, in fact, not in the least romantic. Neither is the drudgery involved in seeing to their needs. Caring for them requires endless patience, tireless energy, sensitive attention over long periods of time. No outsider, like myself, is in a position to dictate where the limits of love lie, or to criticise those who find caring for the handicapped an insupportable burden. But it is astonishing how often they draw out from others, especially their parents, hidden reserves of patience and affection. How we treat them seems in some wise our own and society's acid test. In them, as in the Child at Bethlehem, we see uncamouflaged the native value of humanity itself—helpless, vulnerable, possessing nothing.

And they have much else to teach. They are fearless; they have no enemies. They are trusting; their world includes no villains. They are loving; they do not doubt themselves. They are ghosts of our lost innocence. Nicky will never build a car, or fly an aeroplane, or balance a set of accounts. But he never stops producing joy and love wherever he goes. He is a year-round Christmas gift, however crumpled his wrapping.

Several times in my recent reading I have been pulled up short by flat assertions that nobody any longer takes religion seriously and that religion is no longer a major influence upon society. They reminded me of a similar statement by a rather grand personage who once declared in my hearing that "Of course there is simply nobody in London during August". They reminded me, too, of a conversation with two journalist friends, for whom I have the greatest regard and affection, who suddenly revealed that they could not credit that anybody who had not left his brains in the cradle could be bothered with religion in any shape or form. On my side, I answered that I equally could not credit that anybody with at least a few cells still flickering in the brainbox could fail to take it seriously. On the instant we were eyeing each other like Eskimos and Red Indians suddenly encountering each other on the open sea.

It is easy to see at least some of the reasons why people can jump to such large assumptions. No doubt it is true that the Archbishop of Canterbury and the Cardinal Archbishop of Westminster cannot thump the Prime Minister's desk and successfully demand that Bingo should be outlawed or a swingeing tax put on the consumption of ice-cream. In no area of public life does the churchman speak the final word, utter the decisive judgment. Did he ever? We have a robust tradition in this country of Church and State warily circling round each other and from time to time exchanging a flurry of blows. And the examples of hierocracies or theocracies at various periods of history offer little encouragement to the view that societies are worse when under lay management.

It is also true that people leading active and varied lives can for weeks and months at a time hear no mention of religion nor ever be pressed to divulge their own beliefs. In many circles, except where people feel particularly secure and unbuttoned, a shadow hangs over discussions of religion as it once did over discussion of money, sex and death. As for having firm beliefs, it is widely regarded as more praiseworthy to hold them unobtrusively than to hold them at all.

It is still a considerable leap from such characteristics of our own society to the conclusion that religion has ceased to matter. That is itself a characteristically insular view. Religion at all times and in all places reaches into the deepest depths of the human psyche and in most parts of the world is still, perhaps, the major determinant of the social order. In Latin America, in Asia south and south east, in Iran, in large parts of Africa, in eastern Europe, in the Middle

East, and on our own doorstep in Northern Ireland, religion has in recent years been a major agent of social change, with profound political and economic effects, and has shown an inexhaustible capacity to inspire people at all levels of society to reexamine critically the meaning and conditions of their existence. Whether or not we always approve of the results is beside the point. The point is that whether its force be regarded as malignant or beneficial, religion is for large sections of mankind a more powerful motivator than the dollar exchange rate, any fashionable political theory, or the lure of material prosperity. That is some force by any reckoning, and we minimise or scorn it at our peril.

Even at home the newspaper view of religion as vicars clinking cups of tea in saucers and old ladies pottering round jumble sales is worlds away from reality. The churchmen may not often capture the headlines but they have larger and more faithful legions at their back than most politicians. In every walk of life there are very many people who go about their cherished religious beliefs about the meaning and duties of mortal existence; not only Christians but as well men and women who live by other great religious faiths. Without much effort I can think of a good number of people at the very top of their profession, admired for their acuity, integrity and devotion to duty, whose faith, calmly held and quietly practised, has shaped their outlook and values fundamentally.

And outside the world of public affairs, there is still that astonishing network of communities, groups and individuals tirelessly engaged in prayer and worship, works of care, compassion and healing, the practice of charity and justice, the self-effacing service of others. It is easy not to notice. Such faith does not seek publicity, it only rarely erupts in crusades, missions and festivals, and then rather clumsily and sometimes comically. But were it suddenly expunged, the quality, variety, and temper of the society we at present enjoy would be radically changed for the worse. Day by day it neutralises at least some of the effects of those corrosive acids, selfishness, cynicism, arrogance and heartlessness, which demean and injure our human dignity and human relationships.

NO ABIDING CITY

According to World Refugee Survey there are at least 16 million refugees and displaced persons in today's world. In Africa, approximately 4 million, in Asia 7 million, in Europe 0.25 million, in Latin

America 1 million, and in the Middle East 3.5 million. Though 3 million of these probably no longer require assistance, there are at least as many, and possibly more, who have not yet been registered. Sixteen million refugees. People driven out of their homes, and often out of their countries, by wars, natural disasters, or by religious and political persecution. Their existence is a terrible symbol of the conflicts which rack mankind, our human incapacity to resolve conflicts by reasoned argument, and the bitterness of political and religious enmities. Their houseless heads are dreadful evidence of sheer human incompetence in relieving their distress. Many are short of food, water, shelter, medical aid, as well as work and education, while governments bicker over their own responsibility, and international organisations over their status.

Refugees touch a primal fear in all of us, the fear of being rootless, homeless, exiled from what is familiar and dear. The territorial imperative is strong. We need to know where we belong, to mark a circle round ground we can call our own. When he is driven from home and all that word implies, the refugee is under the sentence of a judgment which pierces the human heart to the quick: "I do not want you. I do not need you. I do not love you." It desolates these innermost regions of the spirit which need the cherishing of affection and regard, brutally hammering to pieces the essential core of self-esteem and cruelly breaking the fragile hold on existence itself. To be driven like leaves before the wind of human anger and contempt, cut off from neighbours and countrymen, to be rendered useless and dependent in strange surroundings and among strangers, surely this is a terrible fate, and it is the fate of the great majority of those 16 million refugees, our kin.

"He took the child and his mother and fled into Egypt." Once again the Gospel presents a Christ who harrows the lowest depths of human experience. We do not know whether Joseph and Mary and the child found a welcome, a temporary security, in that strange country; or encountered suspicion and hostility and lived in wretchedness. But we do know that like all refugees they felt at a loss, and bewildered, and very afraid, and pined for home, because they could not do otherwise. And that in every refugee today, driven into exile, there is something of Christ, and that in Christ there is understanding, born of experience, for the refugee.

Sixteen million refugees. A small fraction of the 250 million people who in the course of this savage century have been refugees. Set against the mountains of dead and wounded who have been victims of the century's wars, or the droves of political prisoners who have

23

been victims of its fanatic ideologies, they may seem relatively lucky. At least they are alive. But the life they live is human existence at its most acid, the very essence of creaturehood—contingent, dependent, impermanent—without any of the sugarcoating with which we disguise the taste of our mortality. That too, perhaps, is why we do not open our arms to refugees. They are too piercing a reminder of what we are ourselves, travelling people who here have no abiding city.

Those countless films and news stories of refugees, their faces stamped with fear and desperation, toiling endless roads to nowhere in particular, of refugees hunted across frontiers like a species of game, of refugees huddled together in squalid settlements, picking away at the idle days while politicians use their lives for barter—all this is a paradigm of the human condition. We know that the most solid house is in truth a flimsy tent, the most celebrated achievement only a scribble on the waters of history, the most outwardly contented and secure existence only a heart-beat from eternity. Even the longest span of life is only a brief touchdown, a fleeting visit, to the kingdom of time.

"Rise, take the child and his mother and go to the land of Israel, for those who sought the child's life are dead." Like Christ, we can at last go home, because by his life and death he has established a home to go to. By love triumphant over sin and death he has driven off all the terrors that are enemies to life; he has revealed the permanent in the midst of impermanence; he has opened the way to a kingdom of joy and security where we can settle for ever. There is hope for all—for the refugees visibly driven from home and country, and for us all, refugees of the spirit seeking our eternal home.

CHURCHMEN AND POLITICIANS

I think it was Tom Lehrer who uttered the immortal remark "I'm against hunger, oppression, poverty and disease—not like the rest of you bums." Stand up everyone who has been (a) embarrassed, (b) annoyed, at catching himself (1) preaching *de haut en bas* or (2) *en bas* and being preached at *de haut*. Now let's all sit down again and reflect together. For unless I am much mistaken, a whiff of holier-than-thouism is causing at least some of the coughing and spluttering on both sides of the nuclear debate within the Church. While it may not be true that Christian killeth Christian, in the course of this argument, Christian certainly scorneth Christian—perhaps the more woundingly because a final judgment for or against the nuclear deterrent is bound to be finely poised, and because the consequence of a mistaken judgment could be so terrible.

With anyone stung by the charge of being a fool or a knave despite painful hours and maybe years of wrestling with the nuclear problem, there should be general sympathy. Where, however, my own store of sympathy rapidly runs dry is at the point where churchmen, lay or clerical, begin to be jumpy at the thought of falling out of step with the State. Disagreeing with that part of the Church opposed to nuclear deterrence is one thing when based on honest argument, quite another when it rests on the belief that one's government is above the Almighty and that some particular party doctrine is the standard of Christian faith.

The cruder expressions of this outlook can be quickly dismissed. If anyone feels that a smile from or a pat on the back from secular authority is enough to make the day, there is nothing to do but call in the priests of the Church and pray that he will quickly recover. And if a church leader nurses that kind of respect for secular authorities it would be best for the Church to insist on his free passage to some uninhabited Solomon Island.

There are, however, plenty of devout Christians, not by nature inclined to tugging their forelocks, who yet feel a tug of loyalties when their faith points in one direction and their political allegiance in another. I say "they" but of course all of us at one time or another can, or do, find ourselves caught in this dilemma; a dilemma most real for those belonging to a church by law established.

Perhaps the dilemma can be put thus simply: the Church is part of the nation but the nation is under God. Here, at a glance, are both sides of the flypaper. The Church and its leaders cannot opt out of the political process, declare UDI from the laws and policies of the government of the day, at least when it has been elected democratically. They, too, are citizens, part of the body politic, locked into the duties and benefits, the failures and successes, of the nation as a whole. Yet their overriding loyalty must be to God and his word, received, meditated upon and acted out within the community of faith. It is their duty to insist that the nation and its government stand, like every individual Christian, at the bar of that judgement, and repeatedly to call attention to the yawning gaps between the divine ideal and the all too human realities.

It is not to be expected, therefore, that churchman and politician should normally be in conjunction. It is a lucky strike if a politician's creed coincides with even a part of the Christian vision. But whether it does or not, once in government the politician is in the power business, intent on directing the national towards certain goals, by persuasion if he can and by coercion if he must. Political creeds touch deep and opposite emotions—yearnings for security or for change and betterment, for tradition or the fresh start, for self-interest or self-sacrifice, for community or independence, for hierarchy or fellowship; that is why they stir passions and almost religious convictions. But all politicians in practice match one set of simplicities against another, and faced with the actual complexities of a spiritually banjaxed world cut all kinds of moral corners to achieve some semblance of order, some hint of forward movement. The Church is a place where the politician, like the citizen, must be able to step out of the wind, to find again the whole vision, the whole truth, and forgiveness for falling short of either. He can expect sympathy, but not too much, for his predicaments, tenderness for his frailties. What he should not expect is whole-hearted endorsement for his policies or a seal of approval for his party. Politics is the pursuit of limited objectives, Christianity the desire and pursuit of the whole. Politics works through manipulation of opinion and pressure for conformity; the Church harbours a spirit restless for truth and reminds us of much the politician would rather forget. The two intersect, they cannot identify. We need politicians who dare to make practical decisions, sometimes right, sometimes wrong. We need churchmen who dare to insist that life is larger than politics, and God grander than governments.

RONALD REAGAN MISCAST

I have just read in a reliable American newspaper that on 13 January 1989, at a banquet in New York, the Knights of Malta awarded President Reagan the order's Grand Cross of Merit Special Class "in recognition of his support of charitable endeavours . . . and his vigorous defense of Christian family values".

Was honour so abused since Caligula made his horse a consul? Have knights made such fools of themselves since the pride of France rode to destruction at Nicopolis?

Such confusion about their faith makes one tremble for the Church. Indeed one accepts that men of affairs cannot be expected to have read the Fathers of the Church, or the works of Thomas Aquinas and Francis de Sales, or waded through Alphonsus Rodriguez on the Practice of Perfection and Christian Virtue. But surely one can expect them to have some passing acquaintance with the Penny Catechism. Or to have skipped briefly through the

Beatitudes. At least one expects them to have a slightly better idea of which way Christianity faces than Jim and Tammy Bakker.

How can we continue to chide prelates and priests for folly when the flower of Catholic chivalry plunges headlong into this nonsense? One understands that there is a smack of ritual, of convention, about such proceedings. One knows that Catholic universities can slip honorary doctorates to all sorts of nefarious characters to attract the favour of the mighty. But at least they honour them as scientists, statesmen, men of letters, not for their shining Christian virtues. If the Knights wished to flatter President Reagan they could have done so as the cheerful charlie who raised the spirits of Americans; as a raconteur; as a fantasist; as the man who ran up the biggest debt in history; or for services to the gravediggers of Central America. But for encouraging charity? For upholding Christian family life? Did they study his treatment of the poor, the homeless, the blacks, the unemployed? Did they test the President's rhetoric against the underlying reality? Did they count the times he darkened a church door? Have they read their Garry Wills? Mr. Reagan may be dear to God, but on the visible human evidence available can he seriously be hailed as a Christian champion? Whatever his virtues, he has certainly caused great distress to many of the poor whom the Church especially cherishes. I have before me a long letter from a jobless, homeless American who has suffered cruelly during the Reagan years. It would draw tears from a stone. I wish I could have read it aloud to the Knights assembled at that banquet. Why is poor Andrew Bertie not dying of shame? And why are these Knights now not doing penance in the desert?

Laugh one must, but can one really laugh it off? Is it not scandalous as well as ludicrous? A scandal for which a supposedly honourable body of laymen have only themselves to reproach. And have the Knights not demeaned the Church as well as blotting their own escutcheons? Perhaps those New York Knights cannot see a chink of difference between the Holy Catholic and Apostolic Church and the Republican Party. But surely there are some Knights who do. Perhaps the New York Knights believe that worldly celebrity is qualification enough for induction into the order. But there must be some who remember that the code of chivalry bade the knight to serve justice, right, piety, the Church, the widow and the orphan. Should that not make them choosy about whom they recruit and whom they honour?

Surely the fact is that the Knights are not to be judged on the same criteria as Shriners or the American Legion. The values they publicly endorse, the people they recruit, the causes they espouse, are interpreted by the wider world as those of the Catholic Church. That requires detachment from fashionable political enthusiasms, resistance to image-making, resistance to the lure of worldly success and power as if these were causes for congratulation in themselves. They cannot appear to value what the Church itself does not value, or incautiously honour what the Church will only rarely, and then with uttermost caution, commend. They cannot afford to commend to Christian regard people who can barely distinguish the Holy Spirit from the Canterville Ghost or the four cardinal virtues from the rules of golf. If Christian applause is sprayed about too freely the Christian Gospel is befogged and believer and unbelievers, rightly, bemused. And that is not a good Knight's work.

EVERY HOUR ON THE HOUR

While visiting an Irish village years ago, my late lamented uncle was invited by the local parish priest to an evening of bridge. There would be, he said, drinks and a sandwich or two at eight o'clock before the game began. Punctually at eight o'clock my uncle knocked at the presbytery door and was ushered in, somewhat hurriedly and abstractedly, by his host. "We won't be a moment, Father," said the parish priest. "Just help yourself to a drink and find yourself a chair." And turning away he rejoined his curate and the local doctor crouched over a small table, absorbed in a game of poker. My uncle seated himself with his drink. Cards were dealt. Hands were played. No words were spoken. Time ticked by.

At nine o'clock the parish priest looked up and said, "Don't be worried, Father, we'll be with you in a moment." As the parish priest's moment already appeared to be a receding horizon, and no food was visible, my uncle reconnoitred the kitchen, found himself something to eat, browsed along the presbytery bookshelves, and settled himself in an armchair with a copy of *Our New Curate*. At ten o'clock there were further reassurances. My uncle took out his rosary and meditated on the mysteries of the Irish clergy. At eleven o'clock he stirred himself to go, but was soothed back into place with earnest apologies and persuasive promises that the bridge would be starting any second.

At six minutes to midnight there was indeed a spurt of furious action. The parish priest slapped down his cards, drew from his pocket a breviary the size of a packet of Swan Vesta matches, canted himself over the side of his chair, and with the miniscule book cupped in his hand inches from the floor, whisked through the pages of Vespers and Compline, finally snapping the book shut with an air of triumph just as the clock struck midnight. Meanwhile the doctor banged down his cards in a fit of pique and complained disgustedly, "My God, you men, you'd think it was Holy Week."

The priest meditatively pacing up and down reciting his office used to be an archetypal figure in both life and literature. There is a fine example in the regimental history of the Irish Guards, where the sight of the late Fr Dolly Brookes, steel-helmeted, quietly walking up and down saying his office during a lively action at a railway station somewhere in France is said to have steadied the troops marvellously. But my uncle's story tells another side to the story. An older generation of priests will recall the days when getting in the office before the bewitching hour of midnight was an obligation hanging daily on the shoulder like an albatross. Just in the nick of time, and another gold star would be pasted in the recording angel's personal file; a moment too late, and the flames of hell danced in the eye.

Recall, too, the casuistry associated with it, the playing with summer time, and double summer time, and international time, that afforded the fly moralist with a flexible conscience any number of midnights from which to choose. Some with little Latin and less Greek will remember the acres of psalms flying by, blurred like a landscape viewed from an express train.

With the modern simplification of the office most of these hazards have been removed and with them a main cause of clerical nervous breakdowns. And a good thing too. It was always the greatest pity that the mechanics of the business, and the dooms attached to the office like limpet mines, drained the pleasure from one of the Church's greatest forms of prayer. Even today they seem to have left a cloud hanging over the exercise. Yet perhaps that regular appointment with the Fathers of the Church and the Scriptures, that regular patrolling of the psalms, which speak to every condition of the human heart and mind, is needed even more today than in ancient times to bring sense and balance into the frenetic activity and deluges of information that make up modern life.

The News. The latterday equivalent of the Church's Hours. At eight in the morning and noon, at five o'clock, and six o'clock, and nine o'clock and ending the day at midnight. Exciting and shocking and disturbing and anxiety-inducing and trouble-making. How it needs that calm counterpoise which follows a slower rhythm and touches more leisurely, deeper themes. And not just for the clergy but for lay people too, the pattern of the Hours makes increasing sense. An antidote to nowness and flatness and one-dimensional living. Regular excursions into the minds that have formed our faith, speaking as often as not about and out of similar conditions, hopes and fears. Regular extensions of our mind's horizons inwards to the mystery of the Trinity, and outwards to all the ills and needs that flesh is heir to. Joining in, every hour on the hour, with the voice and heart of the people of God, as it tunes into and praises, reflects on and thanks, implores and reproaches, delights in and takes heart from, its maker and redeemer. Every hour on the hour drawing on old things and new. Every hour on the hour bringing only good news.

TWO FACES OF GOD

When journalists periodically sniff the air and speculate whether there really is a God at work behind the human scene, they tend to go hunting after dramatic signs and wonders. Was it God who set fire to York Minster? Is it God who sabotaged the Chernobyl reactor and released that radioactive cloud to drift over our heads? No matter 2,000 years of Christianity. The moving finger in the Old Testament writing *mene, mene, tekel, upharsin* on Belshazzar's palace wall, or Zeus casting his thunderbolts from Olympus, make better copy than a still small voice or a God who cooks fish for his disciples on a lakeside fire. Yet among the singular features of Christianity is the bringing of God down to earth, of finding him in all occasions, times and places, and of treating him almost simultaneously with the reverence due to the *mysterium tremendum et fascinans* yet with a curious comfortable familiarity. He is a God whose grandeur can drive believers to their knees, like Peter, stuttering "Depart from me for I am a sinful man", yet also the God with whom Adam walked at ease in the cool of the evening.

Oddly enough, it is the casual side of this relationship which seems the harder for non-believers to accept. I believe it was H.G. Wells who once said that if Catholics genuinely believed in the real presence of Christ in their churches they would go up the aisles on their knees. That they do in fact amble about at their ease, whisper and chatter and laugh in that sacred presence, instead of being as stiff and grave as courtiers attending a renaissance prince, seemed to him an evidence of insincerity.

On the contrary, my own experience—not, I think, uncommon—was that nothing made God so real as this intermingling of familiarity and awe, the holy and the human. And it impressed itself in a variety of ways. As children we lived for long periods with my grandmother, ailing and housebound and unable to get to church. Every week the priest called to hear her confession and bring her communion. These were solemn occasions, and when we were very small children they were heard rather than seen. Very early in the morning there would be the click of the front door as the priest let himself in. A muttered blessing for all dwelling in the house. Then the quiet tread on the staircase leading to her bedroom. An antiphonal exchange of prayers as my aunt and uncle met him at the head of the stairs. The creak of a door. And then voices cheerfully raised as the priest departed, no longer carrying the sacrament in silence, but exchanging jokes and gossip and slipping on bicycle clips and wedging on his huge black hat before leaving. Later I was admitted to the mysteries and saw the small table laid out beside my grandmother's bed, upon its snow-white cloth a crucifix and two small gleaming silver candlesticks with lighted candles, a card with the ritual prayers, a fingerbowl for the priest to wash his fingers and some cottonwool to dry them. And in the bed my grandmother in her voluminous nightgown, a shawl round her shoulders, rosary beads clasped in her fingers, and herself comfortably tucked up in crisp, linen sheets, among crisp plump pillows, and the fragrance of lavender tantalising the air. In such a context "God has visited his people" seemed no distant proclamation but an everyday reality; a God moreover who filtered in and through the commonplace, a God awesome indeed but at home with jokes and gossip and household business.

There was also Brother Alphonsus. He was one of the several de la Salle brothers who lived in the town and taught at a local school for boys. He was a tall bony Lancashireman, cheerful and practical and an elegant football-player, who gave all his spare time to running the scouts and cubs. In summer we mustered behind the school, in a conservationist's delight of a meadow, where he taught us scoutcraft, football and cricket, campfire songs and somewhat dotty dances based on Kipling's *Kim.* In winter we crowded into a dusty attic where the evenings ended with him sitting by a flaring gas fire, in the dark, telling us ghost stories and tales of Sherlock Holmes. To us he knew all that needed to be known, could do all that could be done, and brought infinite delight. He rarely if ever preached. But at the evening's end, in meadow or attic, he would pray with us as we stood sweaty and dusty and exhausted by excitement. He would join his hands and close his eyes fast tight, and speak with profound reverence in his round Lancashire tones, with such earnestness, such intensity of faith, that it seemed possible to reach out and touch the God he was speaking to. Here too, in such an improbable setting, it came easily to believe in a God who

31

delighted to be with the children of men, who was awesome yet somehow humble, who was so at home with us that we could feel at home with him. Not much for a theologian to build on; but echoes, perhaps, of the God who was not out of place at weddings and banquets, and a foretaste of laughter in paradise.

THE NEW CLERICALISM

The newspapers these days seem full of intemperate outbursts by professional football players, aimed at opponents or referees. Most seem boringly uncreative. Certainly none rivals in majestic absurdity an outburst I once heard on the football field at Heythrop in a match between the Theologians and the Philosophers. In the former, older team, were a few players newly ordained and still a trifle self-conscious of their changed status. One of them—now with the angels—was making a beeline for goal when his legs were scythed from under him by a ruthless young fullback. He gradually untangled his limbs, wound himself upright, and puce with anger thundered: "Have you no respect for my sacerdotal dignity?" It almost ended the game, for no one within earshot could run for laughing.

This merry moment came to mind when a priest friend opened a new vista of horror by casually describing a new kind of clericalism. Today's seminarians, he observed, had by and large cast off the old kind of clericalism. They were at ease in or out of clerical dress, expected no special respect or favoured treatment, were not self-conscious of their special status, and had no inclination to patronise the laity. However, he went on, it seemed to him that in another sense they were more clerical than their much-maligned predecessors. Their interest was focused almost exclusively and far more narrowly on subjects—theology, ascetic teaching, liturgy, counselling, of direct professional use to them as priests. Their interest in "secular" subjects was small, and sometimes non-existent. And together we lamented that this development was not the good thing it might appear.

Well, perhaps the sample was small and not typical. And perhaps it might be argued that older generations of priests and religious took their strictly professional disciplines too lightly. But leaving out of account the extremes of the spectrum—the priest unsullied by any kind of knowledge except the knowledge of God and the human heart, and the learned *abbé* beloved of novelists more at ease in the *salon* than in the sanctuary, or the priest who, asked about God, diverts the conversation rapidly to golf—there does seem a smack of danger about turning spirituality into a specialism and priesthood into a craft. Not because there is no science of spirituality as such or because priests do not have their own professional skills, but because of the special and curious character of Christianity itself.

The point might not be so important if such a weight of example and symbolism were not laid upon those formally dedicated to the service of God, but since it is, it does matter that the example and symbolism should signal that the entirety of human interests and activities, except those blatantly sinful, are a delight to God and the stuff of holiness. And that being "spiritual" is not just another compartment of human life like being athletic or good with figures. Looking back, it was a lucky lesson in itself, to be taught by or to come to know religious who were classicists, physicists and mathematicians, lawyers, architects and doctors, farmers, builders and motor mechanics — even diplomats and civil servants, who played games and pursued hobbies, who taught philosophy through *Alice in Wonderland,* and unfolded the mysteries of redemption with the help of Shakespeare. As a tyro Jesuit it was a grace, like many graces resisted at the time, to be led on excursions into anthropology, atomic physics and experimental psychology, as well as biblical exegesis and patristics; and to have superiors who did not think that students of Old Norse, the Shakespearean theatre or forestry were doing work with no relevance to the building of the Kingdom. It was a very lucky lesson indeed to be among people the point and purpose of whose lives was as clear as daylight but who drew down no iron curtain between religious and secular activities.

"I will not take you out of the world." There are depths and depths to that phrase. The Lord himself was a carpenter for most of his life before he began to teach and prophesy. They were not wasted years, and a theology and spirituality that could not take them into account would be a rum business. Indeed a theology and spirituality not constantly being fed by and working upon the whole range of human experience, interest and activity would be a rum business. The curious thing about Christ is that in him God became a very real man. And the curious thing about Christianity is that it does not isolate the sacred from the profane, but makes everything creaturely sacred. It may seem odd to say that priests and religious playing rugby or running a railway club were demonstrating the Christian faith as effectively as preaching from the pulpit, but so I think it was. And I would dread the day when either, hearing the name of Socrates or Mickey Mouse or Arnold Palmer, could only ask blankly, "Who he?"

If I were accosted by a reporter and asked, "What message have you for the Church on the issue of sex and marriage?" I would reply, "Two words. They take in everything. Say nothing." And if he pressed me to explain this curious utterance I would add. "At least say nothing for another 50 years. Let's have a moratorium on the subject for at least that long. Not a word, not a cheep, from popes, bishops or clergy for two or three generations, just to clear the air."

I realise, of course, that the price of taking this advice would be high. Whole departments in the Vatican would have to close down, any number of hardworking *monsignori* in the Holy Office be put out of business. Countless favourite sermons would need to be mothballed. And a large number of reporters on tabloid newspapers would suffer nervous breakdowns, cut off like heroin addicts from a rich source of supply. It may be objected, too, that with the AIDS virus shivering the world's nerves this is no time for the Church to relapse into coyness.

However, the proposal would not be based on the belief that the Church has nothing useful to say on these weighty matters, or be meant to discourage the quiet and effective work of such bodies as the Catholic Marriage Advisory Council or pastoral support for those afflicted with AIDS. It would cover only official public pronouncements from encyclical letters down to the humblest pulpit and its purpose would be strictly evangelical.

The reasoning behind it is thus. First, that the Church, or at least the Catholic Church, is now, in the public mind, identified with sex as village greens with cricket and eggs with bacon. As the word Catholic once automatically prompted the thought "fish on Fridays" now it provokes the words "sex and marriage". However unfairly, for these matters are, as the stock in trade of newspapers, novelists and comedians amply illustrates, of universal interest, they are regarded as the leading and indeed obsessive interest of the Church. Secondly, that continual pronouncements on these subjects have begun, especially in the eyes of the young, to act like interference on a television screen, blurring and obscuring all that lies behind them and, just like such interference, prompting an impatient urge to switch off. Thirdly, that the outbreak of authoritarianism which we are at present witnessing — scarcely a week passing without some new Roman sortie against bishops and theologians reputed to have stepped out of line — and from which the resulting damage far outweighs the intended gain, focuses almost exclusively on issues of sex; issues, perhaps one must add, on which sometimes one leans to the radical side, sometimes the conservative.

Yet from all this huffing and puffing I really do wonder how much good is actually achieved. There is no matter on which it is easier to mount a moral high-horse, nor any on which good advice is least heeded when most needed. Even, I wonder, whether after 2,000 years of hulking cartloads of moral exhortation, human behaviour has altered in practice more than a degree or two. But practical results are the lesser consideration. The greater is whether so much concentration on one area of human behaviour is not drowning out the proclamation of the mighty mystery of redemption itself. Or to put it more graphically, what effect can all this moral exhortation have on people who no longer know the meaning of Christmas and Easter? Insiders may know that the gospels are about the life and death of Jesus Christ and their meaning for the whole of creation; that the life of the Church is about the knowledge, love and worship of the God revealed in Jesus Christ; that Christian literature and preaching from the early fathers onwards have been the unfolding of these mysteries; and that in all of them exhortations on the nature of sex and marriage occupy only a tiny part. The real priorities of the Church need to be reestablished in public understanding, its inmost nature and role expressed without distraction, the sharing in its life of prayer and worship become again the common experience. Hence this not entirely mischievous plea for a self-denying ordinance, 50 years of silence after too much noise, 50 years to rediscover that the Church is not just an ethical society or a school for the reform of manners.

THE MANY-SPLENDOURED THING

"Two voices are there: one is of the deep; and one is of an old half-witted sheep.... And Wordsworth, both are thine." James Stephen's judgment on our greatest romantic poet could, I sometimes think, be applied with equal aptitude to the Church. Institutions, like poets, have their good and bad moments, but surely the Church leads the field in its ability, almost in the same breath, to speak the most sublime truths and to utter flat banalities. The voice of the deep speaks of the grandeur of God, a God whose light is brighter than a thousand suns, whose power holds and moves the stars in myriad galaxies and yet can touch the human heart with the delicacy of a spider's thread, whose Word issues in uncountable

35

and rare species of living creature. A God illimitable, immense, impenetrable, who yet is personal and has left the impress of his nature on every human being born into the world. The more we grasp even a fraction of the immensity of God, the more the fact that he enters the human arena, hangs on a cross, contains himself in a small wafer of bread, can fairly shatter us to pieces. No comment is possible except the Ah-ah-ah, Lord, of the prophet.

This, the vision which the Church keeps before our eyes, is the key to our own dignity, the framework of our existence, the cypher that unscrambles the mystery of our being. In the light of it our strange earthly surroundings become a home, the multitude of our fellow creatures one family, the earth and all its inhabitants our responsibility, and our own trifling personal existence a matter of huge import. For the God the Church speaks of with such frighteningly familiar knowledge is personal, open constantly to communication, intimately affecting and bound up with our spirit and our daily life, the source and the perfect expression of that capacity to love which is man's chief delight, chief glory and chief mystery.

This is the message which the Church has treasured and passed on since its foundation, and whose truth has been tested and found resonant in generations of Christian lives. It is what holds and has held together a body which in any normal judgment could never have come into being. It is the secret of its continuity, consistency and magnetism.

Yet side by side with that tremendous message which irradiates the whole of life is a jumble of nostrums, dictums and instructions which reek of human silliness and reveal nothing except the human incapacity to live with too much grandeur. The awesome and awesomely loving God revealed by the prophets and in Christ is diminished to a clumsy caricature of our own worst selves: petulant, vainglorious, vindictive, pettifogging. Fretted by the daily exactions of the freedom we have been given, we re-write God so that we can cocoon ourselves in rules and regulations and sink gratefully back into irresponsible slavery. Faced with the incredible carnival of life, the amazing variety of cultures, myths, discoveries and expressions of the human spirit, which reflect the inexhaustible fertility of the Creator, we try to concoct a single blueprint for the living of a human life, and attempt to regulate the complexities of human behaviour with the stick-on simplicities of a governess in a Victorian nursery. We escape from faith into superstition, from grace into do-it-yourself salvation more satisfying to our vanity, from freedom and responsibility into the security and dependence of laws and codes. We filter the glazing grandeur of God to a pale,

36

refracted light which will not strain our eyes. We begin in acknowledging God as our ruler, and end in making rules our God. We begin with a sense of wonder and end stifled in bureaucracy.

This I write because a kind but puzzled correspondent asks why I lean to the liberal rather than the conservative version of Catholicism, and express unhappiness at cut and dried answers to problems of human behaviour. It is a first attempt at an answer, emotional perhaps rather than coldly reasoned. But the essence of my objection to Catholic conservatism is its pettiness. The beginning and end of religion is to catch and keep a sense of wonder at the grandeur of God, the grandeur of creation, the dignity of the human being. A mentality that thinks it, or the Church itself, has God in its pocket, that there is only one ideal social order, one ideal pattern of behaviour, one road to paradise, belittles God and is a lie against the richness of creation. The ways in which man understands God, responds to God, worships God, are infinitely subtle and various, as are the ways of human love. Every human life is a profound mystery, and so too the workings of the spirit in each individual soul. The passion for order, conformity, discipline, not as occasional crutches to our weakness but as dominant values sells that richness and subtlety short. We are mysteries proceeding from mystery and living in the midst of mystery. When we think we have God or our own nature taped we have, I believe, abandoned the true pain and excitement of religion and settled for a handy form of social organisation.

TRUTH BEFORE OBEDIENCE

In theory, and often enough in practice, the duty of discretion is bred in the English bone. Sneaks and blabbermouths are not held in high regard. Yet sneaks have their uses, as every policeman knows; gossip is widely relished, as every newspaper knows; and as every schoolboy quickly discovers, an unwillingness to sneak offers him only a limited defence. Giving away the boy who has let loose a mouse in the classroom will lose him his friends; but refusing to reveal schoolmates injecting heroin or running a protection racket will land him in hot water.

This untidy picture becomes untidier still where professional obligations impose a duty of discretion. Doctors, lawyers, journalists, civil servants all find themseles practising a habit of secrecy not only as a matter of justice and loyalty to their clients and superiors, but because without it their business would grind to a halt. Once they can no longer be trusted they might as well shut up shop. Yet this sense of obligation is generally so strong, and strongest of all among the most honourable of men, that it can become their Achilles' heel, for they come to believe that it allows of no exclusions, is indeed an absolute principle. And that way dreadful consequences may lie.

If in this age of murder, genocide, oppression and sinister intrigue, its prophets—such as Primo Levi, Alexander Solzhenitsyn and Hannah Arendt, to mention only a few—have one simple message, it is that wickedness thrives on the silence of otherwise conscientious men and state wickedness on the incapacity of state servants to recognise when the limits of professional duty and habit of discretion must be overridden by the duties of the human being and the enlightened citizen. It could not be right, and it was not accepted as a legal defence, that Germans with secret knowledge that trainloads of Jews were being taken to extermination camps could plead professional obligation for keeping silent, or that soldiers could take part in the murder of the innocent by pleading obedience to their superiors. In no walk of life, with the single exception of the priest, can an absolute obligation of discretion be either imposed or accepted; and the priest is unique because, strictly when hearing confessions, he is acting as the ear and mind of God.

The idea that the duty of discretion must be less than absolute even among state servants is not popular with governments of any description. Yet it is a vital defence against acts of wickedness, or stupidity resulting in wickedness, to which any government may be tempted: most vital of all where governments are most authoritarian, most unyielding in their convictions, and most sure of their own rectitude. They, no less than individuals, cannot rule out the possibility of engaging, culpably or inculpably, knowingly or unknowingly, in acts of wickedness, or equally of being subject to self-interest blinding them to acts of folly. Even the best of governments, the least likely to abuse their power, cannot be accorded a degree of trust that no wise man would place in himself.

Loyalty and discretion are splendid virtues. But even they can be angels of darkness disguised as angels of light. Discretion about what? Loyalty to whom and to what? Conflicts arise, and government or party interest cannot make absolute claims over their resolution. A system of referral outside such interests would be a considerable step towards minimising conflicts of loyalty and guarding against real treachery or individual self-indulgence or bad judgement. But at the end of the road there are still personal, human responsibilities to God and humanity, to the truth, to the public interest, to the requirement of democracy that people should know as fully as can be who and what they are voting for, which sometimes must take precedence over professional discretion and loyalty. This century has suffered not from too little secretiveness but from too much, not from too many revelations of dark deeds, but from too few.

LIVING WITH IMPERFECTION

During the Easter ceremonies this year I found myself haunted by, well, not quite ghosts but absent friends who sometimes seem like ghosts of yesteryear. We all know them. Men and women who, ten, twenty, thirty years ago seemed to have the message of the Council written in their hearts, and bubbling with enthusiasm threw all their energies into translating that message into living reality. The livest wires in parish and student groups, whether their matter was prayer, liturgy, theology or good causes; the pioneers in ecumenical ventures; the people who got their coats off to help every kind of unfortunate; the people who left home and careers to put themselves at the service of the poor in the Third World; the young men and women who took the cause of justice and peace to their hearts. A new breed of laity, the hope of the regiment, the pride of the side. And now, so many of them detached or semi-detached from the institutional Church; at best nursing a private spiritual life, at worst retired into a chilly agnosticism.

Not all, of course not all, but my goodness how many. How many who no longer join in the Easter mysteries or think of themselves as part of the Easter people. And why? Well, who can read hearts; but ostensibly and by their own account because they were drenched by too many buckets of cold water; because they were blunted by too much clerical indifference and lay inertia; because formalism and legalism and protocol still seemed to count for more than palpable human needs; because what to them was Pope John's clarion call to throw open the Church's windows was to so many others more like an air raid warning; because in modern as in ancient Rome, while those at the back cried "forward," those at the front cried "back."

To suggest that any common link exists between the drenchers and the drenched, between the Church's present policy-makers and these disappointed enthusiasts, may seem tiresomely perverse. But so I think there is. It is not that life at the top is more encouraging. Quite the reverse. Rome is in an ugly mood and the new Ultramontanism presents an ugly face to the world. Every *ratissage* against bishops who refuse to be doormats, theologians who raise awkward but unavoidable questions, prophets and heroes who risk their lives to champion the poor in hard deeds as well as glib words, is a shame and scandal. Sometimes there appear to be two Vaticans, the one persecuting whoever lives what the other preaches. In the present atmosphere one needs to pinch oneself to remember that *Ein Befehl ist ein Befehl ist ein Befehl* is not an article of the Catholic faith but the inglorious motto of the SS; that the Church is not a counter-totalitarian party with God at its centre instead of Karl Marx; that the most telling image of the Church is an untidy caravan straggling across the desert, not a parade of infantry goose-stepping across Red Square. There is much to be disheartened by as ecclesiastical power appears to be rated higher than sensitive service, and doctrine and discipline become ever more clearly enmeshed with extreme right-wing politics.

Disheartened perhaps, but not disillusioned. And it is here that the two mentalities described appear to reflect each other. Their characteristic visions of the Church may be very different, indeed poles apart. But the flaw common to both is an incapacity to live with the imperfections, untidiness, tensions and conflict which have always been and will continue always to be an inescapable feature of the Church's life. The one finds it hard to endure the abuses of over-rigid, insensitive church bureaucracy, the other even the appearance of dissent, disagreement and independent initiative. But at bottom both are sighing after a perfect Church which simply cannot be.

The Church is not a clean well-lighted place where everything runs smoothly and actions automatically match ideals. It is in the words of the Gospel a field of cockle and wheat growing up together and beyond human power to separate. The enthusiast will always be running up against rigidity of mind, narrowness of vision, stoniness of heart; no great development in the Church has ever received a fair wind from the start. The lover of good order, of uniformity and discipline will always be confounded by a spirit that blows where it will, by the sheer complexity of human situations and individuals, by prophets and visionaries and non-conformists who cannot be regulated like alarm-clocks. Whether one aches for a Church of inspired whole-hearted enthusiasts or a Church where everyone sings perfectly in tune, one aches in vain. It will always be untidy and riddled with contradictions. It will always have a dark side as well as a bright. Its hidden life will always be more enriching and reassuring than its public demeanour. It is after all the People of God. And people are imperfect and contradictory. To know it we have only to look at ourselves.

HEARERS OF THE WORD

My late revered uncle, for whom God be praised, was, like most veteran parish priests, inured to a certain lack of detectable response in his congregation, no matter how profound his thoughts, how powerful his rhetoric, nor how discriminating his choice of quotations from Aquinas, St Bernard and Alphonsus Liguori. Like so many generations of preachers, week after week, year after year, he looked down upon rows of inscrutable faces, closed eyes and nodding heads, and heard only by way of reply an occasional ambiguous outbreak of coughing which might equally signify either dissent or an outbreak of 'flu.

Imagine, then, his astonishment and delight when one memorable Sunday he looked down from the pulpit and, instead of the usual panorama of ladies hats and bald heads, found himself looking into two alert, intelligent eyes fastened with every indication of fixed attention upon himself. They were, it is true, almond eyes and set in a large round Chinese face. But no matter. An audience is an audience, and a vast improvement upon a mere congregation. Still better, the Chinese not only listened but responded. When my uncle spoke in hopeful accents of heaven and salvation his listener beamed with pleasure; and when he spoke sadly of sin and death the man looked mournful. At frequent intervals he nodded his approval—always heartening for a preacher—or, catching my uncle's mood, shook his head reproachfully over the condition of mankind. The end of the sermon was greeted with a positive volley of smiles and approving nods, and my uncle went into breakfast feeling that for once his wit and wisdom had been properly acknowledged.

Greater still was his pleasure the following week when the Chinese gentleman reappeared, and again the week after, each time achieving new heights of listenership and of course drawing the best out of my uncle. The more he found that, so to speak, shot for shot was returned across the net, the more subtle the strokes he essayed. Into his sermons when Latin tags from the schoolmen, plangent prayers from Newman, daring references to Jean-Paul Sartre and Freddie Ayer, an occasional headline from *Osservatore Romano*. It was heady stuff. But the oriental, with vigorous nod and flashing smile, was equal to it all.

But who, you ask, was this man? And so, of course, did my uncle. When his admirable collaborator showed up for the fourth consecutive Sunday, he took care to be at the church door at the end of Mass and collared him as he came out. How pleasant it had been to see him, he said, and what was his name and where did he come from and would he care for a cup of coffee in the presbytery? The guest nodded and smiled and bowed and said not a word—at least not a word of English, for not a word of English did he know. And this rude shock was not the last. Neither, as inquiries through an interpreter (my uncle was a resourceful man) later revealed, was he a Christian, still less a Catholic. He had simply found the church a warm and companionable place to be. And he had only been waiting for a bus.

Well, that is the story as my uncle told it. And told it to warn against pride in the pulpit and the danger of judging by appearances. But I tell it to suggest that if many preachers seem listless, and they do, and many sermons seem threadbare, and they do, perhaps what the preachers most lack is such a listener. Since clapping in church of popes and bishops is now the rage, and handshakes with fellow-believers acceptable ritual, perhaps we might add to such lively courtesies a sign of encouragement for priests in the pulpit: an occasional thoughtful nod of agreement, an approving smile, even perhaps a discreet upping of the thumb. They might work wonders.

True, direct protests are rare in church, though I remember a man, admittedly lacking a full set of sails, who leaped to his feet during a sermon, and shook his fist towards the heavens and roared "It's lies, lies, it's all lies" before being politely escorted off the premises. More common is the protestor who rises from his seat, makes a steely bow to the pulpit, and marches out like a grenadier, leaving questions troubling the air. The effect is heightened if he is followed by his wife and at least six children. But apathy is discouragement enough, a routine absence of heartening words except from pillars of the parish, who hardly count. As the Chinese gentleman demonstrated, understanding is not essential. All the preacher needs is some indication that he is among the living not the dead, and that some at least are glad to see him. Perhaps, after all, he was an angel with a message: that if preachers are bad, bad listeners make them so.

THE HABIT OF PRAYER

When my maternal Irish-German grandmother died many years ago, perhaps the most touching personal possession she left behind was her old and battered prayerbook. We had lived with her for some years in the early days of the war and the sight of it conjured up a domestic scene as familiar and regular as the rising and setting of the sun. Every evening, when the household tasks were done, she would sit in a high-backed chair and, quietly detaching herself from whatever bustle was going on around her, begin her routine of evening prayer; an invariable set of prayers read from her prayerbook, the rosary, and a few minutes when she would sit, with eyes closed and lips moving silently, making up her own special prayers for the end of the day. The prayerbook she left behind was an eloquent testimony to this daily habit of stretching over heaven knows how many years: stuffed with holy pictures, death cards, fragments of prayers and poems that had taken her fancy, notes of birthdays and anniversaries; and more strikingly still, the pages worn almost to gossamer, some quite tattered and blackened and worn away, by a lifetime's fingering.

In our own home my mother followed the same practice, and had the same gift of sliding unobtrusively out of the surrounding activity and unself-consciously slipping into her private world of prayer. I do not remember any of us ever remarking on either figure, or paying them any attention, still less modifying our own activities to give them special quiet and space. Or, for that matter, either of them ever asking for any. The sight of them at prayer was too familiar for notice or comment. Yet all these years later no scene seems to have impressed itself so indelibly on my memory or made such a lasting impact. It made prayer so strikingly part of normality, an activity as much a part of domestic routine as cooking, washing up or homework, instead of something reserved for church or even one of the disciplines of childhood like morning and night prayers.

Oddly enough, our one excursion into formal family prayer was a failure. Under the influence of a silver-tongued American priest, Fr Peyton, who at one time went round the country crusading for the family rosary—"The family that prays together stays together" was his slogan—we did for a few weeks attempt to follow his advice. The experiment soon collapsed, sabotaged by teenage embarrassment and compulsive fits of self-conscious giggles, not to mention the sheer difficulty every large family experiences of gathering all its members together at one time of day without the aid of lassos and grappling irons.

Perhaps if it had succeeded we would only have carried away a resentful disgruntlement with forced piety, a legacy frequently—though not always persuasively—adduced by adults to vindicate lapses from the faith. The silent witness of one's parents—for my father had his own equally unobtrusive and regular, though different habit of prayer—practising prayer as an unremarkable and entirely normal element of ordinary life, was a gentler and more effective lesson, better calculated to make its mark than any amount of dragooning or exhortation.

Similarly, I later came to think that in a religious community it is not talks about prayer, however, profound, or talkers about prayer, however eloquent, who make the greatest impact, but the priests or brothers or nuns, especially the elderly who have been sticking at it for decades, who are often to be caught unobtrusively at prayer. Every community has such people, people who drift as naturally into prayer as others in quiet moments might pick up a book; and every wise community values them like visiting angels. Quite a few religious, I suspect, will be surprised when the recording angel chalks up the example they have given and the influence they have had in what they themselves regard as undistinguished lives.

Likewise again, I fancy that the kind of parish—now perhaps less common than it used to be—where people seemed all day to be dropping into a church like bees dropping into a hive and where the benches always seemed to be dotted with people praying quietly, and just occasionally not so quietly, commended and developed the habit of prayer better than any number of more self-conscious and stagier events that urge the benefits of prayer with all the subtlety of a loaded shotgun. Next to seeing how Christians love one another, seeing Christians praying as naturally as breathing is perhaps the most appealing and persausive of all the ways in which the knowledge and practice of the faith are passed from generation to generation. And, upon my grandmother, it doesn't cost a penny.

GOING TO CHURCH

Travelling up and down and this way and that across the country during recent months I find myself suddenly surprised by the difficulty of locating a Catholic church. Once away from familiar territory and the comfortable sound of the parish bell, finding a church is, if you will pardon the expression, the very devil. For every church set on a hill there are at least a dozen hidden under a bushel, or at least buried away up a back alley, or screened by trees or behind wire netting. Locals look blank at the mention of the Catholic Church. The telephone number of the church skulks behind the name of the parish priest, which of course you don't know. If by astounding cunning you find it out, he isn't in. Hotels appear to be reserved for Anglicans and post only the services of the Established Church.

But supposing, against these mounting odds, a church is found and, even oddlier, found to be in business. What then? Will the stranger's ears be assaulted by an umpteenth rendition of "Koom by Yah," his eyes amazed by a *corps de ballet* on the sanctuary, his muscles stretched by liturgical PT, his sensibilities scarified by readings from Karl Marx, his senses left reeling by a massed orchestra of triangles and guitars, or any other of the horrors which Archbishop Lefebvre inveighs against and which drive devout agnostics to write protesting letters to the *Listener*?

No, gentle reader, all is quiet on the western front. The second Vatican Council has come and gone but the peace that passeth understanding still rests upon our churches. The stranger sees as he would have seen throughout the centuries a venerable priest, ineffably tired, shuffle onto the sanctuary though now, as often as not, without that mainstay and support, an altar-boy. Now, as then, though in English, he will hear the Mass recited in a flat monotone. The readers are not priests, nor even men, but now as then inaudible. The sermon also is inaudible, and if rarely not, then transcendentally dull. The congregation sits in a stupor, only occasionally revealing that we are among the living not the dead by a cough or the small drama of the collection. Only once, at the kiss of peace, a gentle wave of animation flows through it, smiles break out, children seize the excuse for a brisk canter round the benches.

Sunday Mass. Reformed, restyled, vernacularised, but the same yesterday, today and forever. But I find myself worrying about the young. How can this hold them, will they not be off like shot rabbits as soon as they're no longer handcuffed to their parents' wrists? I worry about non-Catholics sampling a Mass out of curiosity. What will they make of it, where nothing is explained, where all is so casual, so matter of fact, so dutifully uninspiring? How can they ever understand the thing that is being done, glimpse the diamond wrapped in this shroud? I worry about the lonely searching for some human warmth, some deed of kindness among these stolid backs, these frozen, inscrutable faces.

A caricature? I do not think so. Only, except in a few bright places, a picture of normality. And easy in such a mood to wonder what is the point of it all? To consider that perhaps the cynics are right who keep reciting like a mantra that the Church is no longer relevant.

Yet, and yet. Even in the stupifying dullness of the dullest Sunday Mass I see and hear a message that is still eloquent even though it speaks through a silence. The sermons may be dull, but they do not tell me to hate, to kill and to grab. They do not preach that

45

large portions of the human race are natural enemies of my country or my class. They do not preach that large numbers of my fellow human beings must die for the sake of some political utopia. They do not say that despite regrettable inconvenience to the public I must insist on my rights no matter what the cost. They do not tell me to lie, cheat and fiddle my way to the top. They do not persuade me with honeyed words to buy things I do not need for a price I can't afford. They do not tell me that if I do not wear the right clothes or know the right people or am underinsured I might as well be dead, man. There are many things I do not hear even in the dullest sermons which are a comfortable kindness. And when I strain to hear those inaudible voices I do in fact hear words more comfortable still, like love and peace and forbearance and forgiveness. I am grateful for that, and grateful to think that, however turgidly, these thin trickles of unselfishness and idealism are every Sunday purifying the bog of everyday life.

In the tired priest and those stolid backs I also see a living model of unselfishness. He as he casually goes about his awesome business, and they as they nod in the benches are by their very presence testifying to a presence greater than themselves, a duty which overrides immediate gratification, a meaning to life that makes sense of all its incident, oddness and botheration. How they go about the great matter of the Mass is essentially of little consequence. The fact that it is done, and that there are people who recognise that, however clumsily, it must be done, and that in the doing all our wounds are healed and our fragmented world made whole, is what really counts. I know that generations of equally casual, equally soporific Christians have sagged in these benches, punctuating idle thoughts with sporadic prayers, and that if there is one certainty about the future it is that other generations will take their place tomorrow. The very lack of show, the absence of polish and public relations, has a terrible confidence about it, a brutal certainty that nothing we can do will ever quite undo what Christ himself has done. Among the damp raincoats, the coughing and sneezing and shuffling feet, among the crying babies, inaudible preachers and self-conscious readers, he has built his tabernacle, because we human beings are like that and need light and warmth in our ordinariness—not in our rare moments of glamour and gallantry.

When two stand together at the altar and vow their lives each to the other they are symbolising one of the most important characteristics of a Christian marriage: that it is open and public. They are publicly proclaiming their love for each other before family and friends and in so doing they express something about the nature of Christian marriage itself.

It is not a secret and furtive thing. It is not an *egotisme a deux*. It is not just a private satisfaction. Christian marriage is the framework of love which is outward-looking, lived in the Christian community for its enrichment and ultimately for the enrichment of all mankind.

Love which can exist only in a secret garden soon finds the world knocking down the walls and breaking in. Only a love which is free, frank, proudly acknowledged, can walk through the wilderness of the world unscathed and bring the wild beasts to heel.   I think it was Antoine de Saint Exupery who said that love was not looking into each other's eyes, but looking together in the same direction. A Christian couple must look outside themselves, be concerned with, and at the service of, others, and in so doing they mysteriously grow together, just as the individual becomes his true self by giving himself away.

The married couple, like the individual, find that in giving, they receive. The style of modern marriage often leads to a contraction of love, a narrowing of horizons and interests, a concentration on material possessions and social status, the making of infinite demands on all too finite persons. It becomes a prison.

Christian marriage means a combining of strengths for the love, service and development of others. It *can* mean, when possible, keeping open house; it *always* means keeping open hearts.

Marriage is ideally a constant loving relationship between two persons. It is also a covenant, a contract, a social institution. These are cold legal words, and they can sound pretty unromantic and even unpalatable. But they express something which is objectively true in the nature of marriage itself, an undercurrent beneath the fluctuations of moods and feelings—that marriage is a bond of faith and faithfulness.

Marriage means to make an act of faith, to pledge faith, to keep faith. And the structure of marriage is rooted in the faith which God, our father and fond, keeps with his human creatures, and Christ with his Church.

Acts of faith are commonplace in everyday life. When a person entrusts a secret to a confidante, business affairs to a solicitor, puts his life in the hands of his doctor, he is making an act of faith in their dependability, integrity and competence. It means handing over something personal and precious. But nothing rivals the act of faith two human beings make in each other on their wedding day. The words 'I will' are then mighty enough to crack the heavens open. It is the greatest compliment one human being can pay to another, this recognition of a quality so unique and so attractive that it inspires each to hand over their whole self to the other, to share the whole of life with all its vicissitudes together. It is an act of faith which moves each to give to the other all that is most intimate and precious in themselves and to expect nothing less in return. And it is an act of faith in the essential goodness of humanity itself, despite all the selfishness, weakness and fragility which mar man's estate. Marriage is an act of faith in the face of cynicism, of hope in the face of despair.

I will take this man, this woman. You, you only, and you always, it says. For better, for worse; for richer, for poorer; in sickness and in health. And not only in the great crises. Despite, too, the petty aggravations that little by little can abrade faith and patience: mannerisms, tricks of speech, conflicts of interest, divergences in temperament.

It is an awful lot to ask. Without the institution to buttress them, perhaps it would be impossible for human beings to keep such faith, even, like the poet, 'in one's fashion'. But that at least signals the ideal to which the married are committed. And in turn the faithfulness of the married represents and points to the faithfulness of God. No matter how seriously we break faith with him, he keeps faith with us. He is the keeper of promises, the changeless one. His covenant is everlasting: 'I shall be your God, and you shall be my people'; 'I will be with you all days even to the consummation of the world'. In grasping the faithfulness of God we learn to keep faith with each other, just as in discovering his love for us we learn to love each other. In the faithfulness of marriage his faithfulness is drawn into human society, and by that divine faithfulness marriage itself is sustained.

Marriage is a union and a communion of selves. It is both the basic unit of human community, the commonest agency through which the divine gift of communion infiltrates human society. A community and communion of which communication is the lifeblood.

It is communication in all its forms which breaks down the barriers behind which what Iris Murdoch calls the 'fat relentless ego' continually seeks refuge. It is communication which finds its delicate way into that dark cellar where self worships at its own shrine. It is communication that coaxes the fearful personality out of sterile darkness where growth and development are stunted, into the light. Looks, words, gestures, touches, all set up a resonance, a path along which even unconscious and inarticulate thoughts, hopes, anxieties and fears can travel. While beyond them lies not the silence of unease which breeds resentment, but the counted silence in which heart speaks to heart and is understood.

Only communicate. So easy in theory, so difficult in practice. It needs calculated effort if two human beings are to wear each other in their heart's core, and not drift apart until they are simply strangers under one roof. Communication requires trust, and to create trust there must be respect for the individuality and freedom of the other. As a marriage develops, the very otherness of the other which was once a source of attraction can so easily become a source of friction. Nobody believes on their wedding day that they are marrying a plaster saint. But as time goes on they may act as if they thought so, or worse still try to fashion one.

Ideally there should be in a Christian marriage neither overlord nor overlady, no place for a Higgins trying to re-make his Eliza according to his own blueprint. It is only in the experience of freedom and individuality mutually respected that we can be tutored in the freedom of the children of God. Constraints, impositions, foster distrust and grudging service: freedom and respect, trusting love. In Chaucer's words:

Love wol nat been constrayned by maistrie.
When maistrie comth, the God of Love anon
Beteth his wynges, and farewel, he is gon!

Only where there is that daily experience of trust and acceptance—even of follies and oddities—can both mind and body, even the most secret thoughts, be given into another's keeping. When communication breaks down it is incredibly difficult to resume normal service: but where there is a steady growth in open trust and open communication, the small weeds of irritation, inevitable as they are, quickly waste away.

Lovers always have the sense of something *given.* They cannot find in themselves an adequate explanation for all that they feel and understand. In the intimate giving and receiving of their love they not only reveal and discover their own truest selves but come face to face with the mystery of human personality, and beyond that to the unplumbable mystery of God himself. The very acceptance and enjoyment of the gift they have received brings them into the presence of the Giver. And the circle is completed when human sexuality, through which the gift of love and a richer life is celebrated, in turn transmits the gift of life to others: a gift because none of us can call himself into being, or demand the right to exist.

Human sexuality hands on love and life. It is also an eloquent language. It can express joy, sorrow, gaiety and melancholy, communicate strength and the desire for strengthening, comfort and the need to be comforted. It may be solemn, reverential, playful, even casual, with the casualness of those whose spirits have drawn so close that they are completely in tune with each other. As such a language, it is arguably the most subtle vehicle for thoughts, attitudes, aspirations, feelings for which articulated words are too clumsy, like sounds pitched too high for the human ear. The scriptures define it by the very 'to know' because it is a path to knowledge, for better or worse, of self and another's self; a knowledge which touches the very quick of self, and detects every deceit and every kind of camouflage.

A language in which the mystery of one person speaks to another. And yet more than that. A language, too, in which God speaks eloquently of himself. Through the expression of love between two mortal, finite, mutable and fragile human beings, a love shadowed by death, there develops the desire of the absolute, a love that is infinite and totally satisfying: and there comes to birth a holy instinct that such longings are made to be satisfied, an instinct that knows unerringly there exists such a love completing human love. In the knowledge of another self there steals into sight the One who made that self; in the experience of human love the Love who moves the planets and the stars.

YOUTH AND AGE

The other day a brochure dropped through my letter-box announcing a conference for elderly people entitled *The Age of Frailty*. "Humph", I found myself grunting. For though the handicaps and disabilities of old age are not unfamiliar, and indeed sometimes seem to have set in before one was out of one's perambulator, it is one of the odder features of modern life that old people seem to be made of tungsten and teak. There is little of the sere'd-and-yellow leafish quality about them. The problem is to keep up as, with apple cheeks and sparkling eyes, with a hop-step-and-a-jump, they leap onto toboggans, gallop over ploughed fields and put in pressing applications for trips to the moon.

They are in fact only one half of a curious equation, that young people seem to be older, while old people seem to be younger, than they used to be half a century ago; though the first half of that equation is more difficult to stomach. I am still trying to salvage my self-respect after taking a young cousin on an outing to the Science Museum. My role of guide and mentor lasted some three or four minutes. After a couple of stumbling attempts to explain some simple machines in the children's section, my cover was blown and our roles were briskly reversed. For the rest of the morning I trailed along behind this precocious 10-year-old trying to catch hold of scraps of information from a continuous lecture on sciences I did not know existed at a level I thought reserved to the Pontifical Academy of Sciences.

Even more demoralising was an encounter with another 10-year-old during the last Christmas holidays. He turned up in a visiting family party and to make avuncular conversation I asked whether his school made much use of computers. O folly. O foolishness! For the next three-quarters of an hour I was given a foundation course in the theory and practice of computers of which I understood *not one word;* well, perhaps the buts and the ands. C.P. Snow's theory of the Two Cultures suddenly struck home as never before. The only effective counter appears to be to brush up one's Latin and to refuse to speak anything else. That fixes them.

But while ever at our backs we hear precocious children hurrying near, the elderly with gathering speed are drawing well ahead of time's winged chariot. Time was when George Bernard Shaw caused wonderment when at the age of 91 he fell out of a tree while picking apples; and W.G. Grace was much admired for continuing to play cricket until well into his sixties. Today's elderly people seem to take such feats in their stride. Not so long ago a relative who has just celebrated her eighty-sixth birthday fell and cut her leg quite badly. She drove herself six miles to the hospital, had the wound sewn up with 14 stitches, and then drove herself home again. But even this feat was eclipsed by an octagenarian lady who lives in our neighbourhood. When she came back from holidays abroad, a friend, thinking no doubt of idle days sipping sherbet beneath a parasol and reading Jane Austen beside the wine-dark sea, asked "And what did you do on your holiday?" "Hang-gliding" she answered dismissively.

The secret of this phenomenon continues to elude me. In a hopeful moment of search I recently fastened on a second-hand book written by an ancient gentleman aged 105, some time in the 18th century, elegantly expressed and full of sound advice for those who wished to follow in his footsteps. The effect was marginally spoiled by a printers' footnote recording that the author had passed away more or less as he had laid down his pen. But what matter? He had sacrificed himself for the good of others. And his message was a simple one: wholesome food, a glass of strong beer at bedtime, and a daily routine of prayer and pious exercises.

For at least some of the ebullient ancients I have in mind as I write, this seems an unlikely prescription. But the last part is undoubtedly sound. There is a story that when a recent pope wished to alleviate the rigours of Carthusian life, the monks asked if they might send a delegation to Rome to represent their views. The pope agreed. When the delegation entered his presence every single member was in his nineties. The order most given to silence had found its own way of staging a silent protest. Prayer is certainly part of their secret. And coming to think of it, I believe they go in for wholesome food too.

THE PATH TO PEACE

Some years ago while browsing in a Toronto bookshop I came across a poem by a poet unknown to me, Robert Tristram Coffin. It was called "Crystal Moment" and in it the poet describes how one September morning a hunt swept past him in full cry. It catches the panic of the stag, the bloodlust of the hounds.

> Fear made him lovely past belief
> My heart was trembling life a leaf.
>
> He leaned towards the land and life
> With need above him like a knife.
>
> In his wake the hot hounds churned,
> They stretched their muzzles out and yearned.
>
> They bayed no more, but swam and throbbed,
> Hunger drove them till they sobbed.
>
> Pursued, pursuers, reached the shore
> And vanished; I saw nothing more.
>
> So they passed, a pageant such
> As only gods could witness much.
>
> Life and death upon one tether
> And running beautiful together.

The last lines have been ticking away quietly in my mind ever since I first set eyes on them. Life and death upon one tether. Not locked

52

in a fierce and ultimately one-sided combat. Not desperate enemies. Not even juxtaposed. But needing each other. Fitted together. And with the passion of life and the horror of death at a point of perfect balance, creating between them an incandescent beauty.

This apparent discord which at a deeper level sounds in harmony is not unique. On every side apparent contradictions find their resolution in some higher unity, apparent conflicts threatening disintegration prove to be a spring of creation. Opposites do balance, do feed off each other. Each in its own way is an umbilical cord for the other. Pain and pleasure. Joy and sorrow. Darkness and light. Each is necessary to the other, interprets it, gives it meaning. "Absence makes the heart grow fonder" says the old saw. Without knowing separation we cannot know the true joy of being together. Without darkness we cannot appreciate light. Without quarrelling, the pleasure of reconciliation. Without frustration, the delight of achievement. It is not too much to say that without experience of the abnormal we cannot plumb or relish any normal condition.

These everyday lessons of life have a bearing, it seems to me, on the Christian understanding of peace. There is an inclination to speak as if Christianity, perfectly practised, would usher in an age free of all conflict and contradiction, a world without struggles, disputes, and trials of strength. But as in the life of the mind and heart, so in social life conflict is embedded in the nature of things, and it is unimaginable that it should be otherwise. If there is an aspect of paradise most difficult to grasp, it is the notion of unrelieved tranquillity, a life without challenge or stress. Here, in the interim, we know that two men cannot stand on the same foot of ground, both teams win the Cup Final, and, as Abraham Lincoln observed, two children cannot claim two out of three available hazelnuts. To wish away conflict is to wish away life as we know it.

If that is so, what is it we mean by "peace" in Christian language, and what would we mean if by a miracle all the guns were silent and all the armies disbanded, and we were simply left to live out our days as men inhabiting a finite world but open to infinite choices? Peace in the Christian sense, I believe, is less the abolition of conflict than the strength to manage conflict. Whether the stress we have to contend with is psychological or social, the power to cope with it, to hold the opposites together, to use the experience of conflict, frustration, antagonism, loss, is a positive grace more to the purpose than the pursuit of a stressless nirvana or even worse the expectation that someday the key will fall into our laps that opens the door into a lotus land where no storms come. Christ himself had a hard row to hoe, but, whether torn by internal conflicts or assaulted by the outside world, he retains an inner strength which enables him to absorb and transmute all the stress into a more penetrating wisdom and an all-embracing love. He does not move in a still world but is the still centre of his world. That, surely, is what Christian peace is about.

The second contribution that Christianity makes to the establishment of social peace is its ability to make proud, truculent men into graceful losers, secure in the knowledge that what to those who do not share the Christian visions is outward loss, is *sub specie aeternitatis* inward gain. To be a good loser seems at first sight a pathetic ideal, and it is easy to mock, but it makes more sense when the reality is squarely faced that in a wide variety of conflicts there have to be losers as well as winners and that not all by a long chalk can be settled by compromise or leave honour satisfied all round. Someone, as often as not, has to back off, and the Christian faith enables those who hold it to back off without feeling that their integrity and self-image are irreparably fractured, or that some loss of public esteem makes their future existence intolerable. When we say "blessed are the peace-makers" it often sounds as if the Christian is always above the battle, neutral in the conflict, the outsider above such things, calling the chaps together and persuading them to make up. The truth is that the Christian is as likely as anyone else to be caught up in every kind of conflict, but a trifle less likely to feel that if he cannot win neither can he live with himself. And the closer to Christ he grows, the easier it becomes to allow the advantage, in whatever is held dear — reputation, possessions, prestige — to the other side. Self-giving matters more, humiliation counts for less. And when the Christian stands his ground, as stand, sometimes, he must, if the world is not to be run by those who have no scruples, he will do so for causes larger than his own immediate and petty self-interest. In a world where so many are consciously dedicated to picking quarrels, and being a loser even at elbow-wrestling is a matter for shame, to have people willing to step off the pavement except in great matters is no bad thing. Humility is not nowadays highly prized, but it is often the only path to peace.

FREEDOM

Freedom, like justice, is never perfect in any human society. We can only talk in terms of more or less freedom. The great political problem of our time, and perhaps of any time, is to balance the claims of fairness and the freedom of individuals. But I have no doubt whatsoever that the mark of a civilised society is to cherish and enlarge the maximum freedom for all, while cushioning the weak against abusers of freedom. And what I value most about this country is the extraordinary extent to which we can say what we please, go where we please and do what we please. And that where laws and rules and regulations seem unreasonably to cramp our style, we can organise and protest against them. It is a freedom that has been painfully won, by wars, political strife, and the sacrifice of brave individuals. It should never be taken for granted.

Freedom is not just a question of politics. The oddest thing about God's creation is that he made men free, knowing full well we would use our freedom irresponsibly and to the destruction of ourselves and others. It would have been so much easier to make creatures who were automatically good. It is a constant temptation for people who have power over others to try and force them to be good. But if we are not free, free to be cruel as well as kind, free to be selfish as well as loving, free to be treacherous as well as honest, virtue has no merit and no value. A human act, said Thomas Aquinas, is an act which is free from interest or external compulsion. To be truly human we must be truly free. The art of living is to strive always for greater freedom, and to learn to use our freedom responsibly.

So far what I have been talking about has been social freedom — freedom to make choices, to speak our minds, to have some say over our own lives. But there is another kind of freedom, freedom of spirit. It is a deeper kind of freedom than simply being able to do as we please.

All my life I have had the great privilege of knowing people who had very little social freedom, but were free where it matters, inside themselves. Paralysed people who could not go where they pleased but depended on others to move them. People who were poor and never saw much of the carnival of life because they had not got the entrance money. People who were handicapped all their lives because they had to leave school too young. Above all, many men and women who suffered for years in the wartime concentration camps of Nazi Germany.

They certainly had no social freedom in the accepted sense. They were not only imprisoned, but systematically starved, often beaten and tortured, forced to do exhausting and degrading work. Deliberate attempts were made to make them feel more like beasts than men. Their faith was tested by the sight of human behaviour at its most vicious and cruel. Their hope was eaten away by the daily spectacle of mass murder. Their love had to rise to the challenge of every kind of treachery, exploitation and selfishness. Yet where everything we value as freedom was lacking they remained spiritually free, free inside themselves.

What does this freedom of spirit mean? First of all not being tied to things so that when they are lost one's self is lost with them. If we depend for our happiness or survival or self-esteem on possessions, money, power, good looks, or anything else that comes and goes, *when* they go there seems no further point to living. Freedom of spirit means being detached from all created things, so that we value them, use them, enjoy them, but do not become their slaves.

Secondly, freedom of spirit means respecting and learning from the opinions of others, but not automatically giving in to them or stubbornly taking no notice of them. It is freedom of spirit to be able to combine with others in friendship, but to resist becoming part of the herd.

Thirdly, freedom of spirit means preserving sufficient clarity of mind to distinguish what is good from what is evil, despite pain and suffering, despite bribes and threats, when it no longer seems to pay and when there is no-one else to look to for support.

Finaly freedom of spirit involves faith. I will not say in God — because not everyone free in spirit believes in my own God, though I suspect they love him in one of his disguises, but in some meaning and purpose to life which makes life itself worth living, human dignity paramount, and human integrity inviolable.

Those who are free in spirit are not just valuable and to be admired in themselves. They are living reminders that the freedom we struggle for outside ourselves, in the conditions of life, is to help us become free inside ourselves. And they are reminders that freedom is to be penetrated by love if it is not to be destructive. Certainly law can step in to control inevitable abuses. Law that is the grudging respect love pays to original sin. But law is a safety-net, not a means to salvation. St Paul tells us that as Christians we must try to be men who do not need law, do not depend on law. Freedom and responsibility. Freedom and unselfish love. That is the Christian ideal. 'Life and death upon one tether, And running beautiful together'.

A PLACE FOR MODESTY

My late uncle, who for much too long has been absent from these pages, came back from his student days in Rome at the Propaganda College in thrall to all things Italian. Thereafter he regarded Italian art, music, architecture, cuisine, and railways as the peak of civilisation and quickly established himself as the artistic conscience of his diocese. And in the fullness of time his fervour embraced the Italian cinema. As each new masterpiece arrived on these shores he would tear himself away from the pages of *L'Osservatore Romano* — Italian edition — and light out for the lone Newcastle cinema which catered for intellectuals. I had, in fact, a sneaking suspicion that but for his friendship with the manager the intellectuals of Newcastle might have had an even thinner time, but while he lived he single-handed kept the standards up and the profits down. Not, however, without occasional wavering on the part of the manager.

It was one such waver that caused him an embarrassing moment. He set out one winter's afternoon, muffled and wrapped against the weather, but inwardly glowing with the prospect of viewing the latest Fellini — "a very good Catholic, I believe" — and in his usual absent-minded reverie stumped up at the ticket office, felt his way through the smoky darkness of the cinema interior, and slipped into a seat. He went through the customary ritual of checking ticket, spectacles, cigarettes and matches, and then looked up at the screen.

He got a shock. The main feature was indeed the latest Italian masterpiece, but the second had a somewhat less classical character and was clearly aimed — the manager had been hedging his bets — at an audience with baser appetites than your average Newcastle intellectual. It was in short the kind of film in which the actors wear little else but smiles. Now a modern curate of advanced views might even relish such a rush of fortune; and a modern conservative curate lightly dismiss any unseemly thoughts with a dash of holy water. But my uncle was of a different generation, a generation trained in the seminary to direct its gaze to the ground and never to look a woman in the eye. Thus the moral dilemma. They were naked, and he was ashamed. What would the Children of Mary, the Catholic Women's League and the Altar Society think of a parish priest who idled away his afternoon in front of a film they forbade to their sons and husbands? And, needless to say, there were bound to be Catholics in the audience.

So, the drama in a nutshell. No doubt an innocent layman, especially a Protestant, would at this point expect the outraged priest to storm out of the cinema, casting withering looks at the manager. But remember. My uncle had been trained by Jesuits; he was an experienced parish priest; and he had paid for his ticket. So what he actually did was to slouch deep down in his seat, pull his overcoat collar up to his ears and his beret over his eyes, and compose himself for forty winks or the start of the main feature, whichever was the shorter. For all I know he may even have been reciting the rosary on automatic pilot. Whatever the case, he was sure he had disposed of the problem to the satisfaction of both his conscience and his pocket. When suddenly, a torch shone full in his face, an usherette bent over him, and a female Geordie voice powerful enough to topple the Tyne Bridge into the river, inquired an inch from his ear, "Are you enjoying the film, Fa-aa-ther?" It was the last straw. He bolted.

Today a story like that sounds like a period piece. The age of such moral niceties seems long past. To confess to even a slight degree of prudery is less socially acceptable than daring to mention a once unmentionable disease. That change of attitude may be good up to a point. A certain robust earthiness seems closer to the spirit of the scripture than the genteel prudishness that used to be commonplace among pious people. It is also true that some of the noisiest spokesmen for "moral standards" and a return to reticence in what we see, hear and read, often lack all discrimination. But reading as I have read within the past week that sexploitation films in central London draw many times larger audiences than the general run of feature films, and that the most vicious and sadistic video-cassettes are being bought and hired in hundreds of thousands, I cannot help feeling that a dangerous line has been crossed. To put it mildly, the thought that many thousands of my fellow citizens actually find some satisfaction in watching holes being drilled in fellow-human beings, or the gang-rape of young women, is both dispiriting and disturbing. For the sociologist and psychologist it raises dark questions. But for us all, perhaps a recognition that there is still some place for modesty, for reticence, for admitting that at some point we can still be shocked, is overdue; and not for motives of bourgeois prudishness, but from Christian reverence for the human person. There is surely a standard somewhere between Mrs Grundy and Soho.

REALITY REVEALED

"Out there," says the chairman, with a sweep of his hand towards the nearest window, "out there is the real world." It is a curious phrase, and all the more curious because everybody seems to use it. Go to any meeting of bankers, policemen, social workers, clergy, academics, doctors, lawyers, soldiers or any other profession you care to think of, and it is even money that within ten minutes someone will be saying "out there in the real world".

Parents, too, are fond of it: "My boy, my girl when you go into the real world..." And teachers: "One day, when you have to face the real world..."

Nobody, it would appear, believes their own world to be real. The real world is always somewhere else. This room, the phrase implies, this occupation, this piece of business, you and I and all present, are not part of the real world. For one group, the real world is the corridors of power or the wheeling-dealing world of high finance. In the corridors of power, the real world is the world of poverty and homelessness, of crime and drug addiction, where life is a harsh struggle to survive. Yet in that very world, the carers and servicers, asked about their aims, answer that it is to get the disadvantaged "back into the real world". Contrary to Keats's view that "nothing ever becomes real till it is experienced", the exact reverse appears to be the case; it is what is experienced that seems trifling, illusory, insubstantial.

Even the priest at the altar is not immune. How often we hear him say as the Mass concludes: "Go forth into the world in peace and joy"—as if the Mass itself is taking place in a time and space vacuum sealed off from the real world beyond the church door, waiting, like some mysterious tundra, to be explored by the emerging faithful. A curious state of mind for Christians whom their master has told "I will not take you out of the world" and who believe that in their central act of worship they come as close to the heart of reality as it is possible to be.

Perhaps this last case is not quite on all fours with the rest, but the phenomenon in general is so curious that it may serve as a starting point for reflection. Is it, I wonder, another of what Peter Berger once called "rumours of angels"?—an expression of a haunting, instinctive sense that we do dwell in a shadowland, a clumsy tribute to an order of being beyond the range of sight, sound and touch, a nagging intuition that literally, if we had the trick of it, we might turn but a stone and start an angel's wing? Are we, when we speak of the real world "out there", edging at some primitive level into the experience of the mystic who finds the veil being twitched aside between the familiar world and another, more vivid, more complete, more stable and more harmonious; where also, often enough, the sense of the presence of God, in normal life so dim and fitful, is heightened beyond expression? An experience, or rather experiences, incidentally that the work of the Oxford Research Institute into Religious Experience indicates are far less rarified than is commonly supposed.

To argue that because we ache for a reality more substantial than the one we know, there must be a reality to fit the ache, has an Anselmic ring and no doubt is open to similar objections. But it may not be a bad hypothesis to work on. The ache itself is real enough, a universal sense that this "false world is but transitory"; of disjointedness and incompleteness; of dealing always in what is essentially provisional. Something in us longs to bang the last nail into place, to add the last coat of varnish, and is yet continually frustrated. We long to reach the world's end and find the horizon continually receding. The real world always lies beyond.

Two elements in the mystic tradition of every great religion speak to that condition. One is the tradition that the real world cannot be found simply by moving house or changing occupation. It lies within. And it is in searching our own inner depths, and by that alone, that we can finally get in touch with ultimate reality. The second is that we cannot by our own unaided power net this ultimate reality, whatever, whoever, it proves to be. All we can do is to prepare the ground, make ourselves receptive, for a revelation which if the business is honestly and patiently done, will certainly be forthcoming. For man cannot wish to know God more than God wishes to be known.

Preparing the ground for that revelation is surely what Lent is all about. The ancient formula of prayer, reflection, penitence, self-denial, is exactly that. The task goes deeper than the reordering of the surface of our lives or even more effective ways of serving our neighbour. For even they, to be wisely done, depend on the knowledge that the real world is never somewhere else but everywhere, and that each of us carries it within.

THE USE OF FORCE

When I first started to go to school I had to pass two rival schools to get to my own. Almost every morning those of us who took the same route found little groups of children waiting for us, spoiling for a fight. We had to fight on the way there, and fight on the way back. Nobody told us to fight, and nobody goaded us to fight. It was a ritual. And it was an instinct. All our lives that instinct to use force on others is at work and there are dozens of motives for it. Sometimes just plain rivalry as it was in the example I have given. Sometimes the desire to be top-dog, and put other people in their place—below ourselves. Or to get our own way. Or because we cannot find the words to settle an argument. Or to take something from others, or to defend something they are trying to take from us. Or just to feel our own power, or to see other people humiliated.

Whatever the reason, the temptation is always there beckoning. 'If you don't do it I'll make you'. Sometimes pretty crudely when the children are creating bedlam and parents have had just about enough. Sometimes silkily, at the business conference or in the Council chamber. Yet two things, I think, stand out about the use of force. One, that it rarely achieves lasting results. And the other that it damages the user just as much as the victim. Two hundred years ago Edmund Burke made the point when he said: "The use of force alone is but temporary. It may subdue for a moment; but it does not remove the necessity of subduing again: and a nation is not governed, which is perpetually to be conquered". He was talking about war, but you could say much the same about force in personal relations. You cannot force plants to grow—only create the best conditions in which they can grow. And no more can you successfully use force on people. The use of force always marks a failure. A failure of imagination, of ingenuity, of love, of forgiveness. And we have only to examine our own feelings when we ourselves are on the receiving end to know the legacy it leaves, and its ultimate futility. When we are forced to do things against our will we do what we have to do just as long as the pressure lasts, we do the minimum we can get away with, and we stop as soon as we can. And what is left behind is steaming resentment, anger, and as often as not the desire to even the score. How many political and industrial troublespots today are the results of a desire to pay off old grudges, a desire to revenge injustices once imposed or perpetuated by force. And contrast those feelings of resentment, reluctance and revenge with the cheerful service of those who love and who feel loved. Nothing seems too difficult, nothing too much, for those who love us and whom we love. So too when we act out of love we feel we have grown in the process, become more completely our true self. Whereas when we use force we are somehow diminished, defeated, less sensitive to the humanity of those we injure, even to the goodness and beauty of the world around us.

'He who takes the sword will perish by the sword'. Christ did not just mean that those who kill will die violently. There is more to it than that. He meant, I think, that we damage or destroy our own nature by acting violently. Love one another as I have loved you. God's love is endlessly forgiving, endlessly patient, endlessly seeking reconciliation, as he described himself in the Book of Exodus:

'A God of tenderness and compassion, slow to anger, rich in kindness and faithfulness'. To be truly men we must be godlike, refusing the short cut of violence, loving beyond reason, forgiving beyond reason, till our love touches the heart of our enemies.

Violent behaviour between nations and between persons is something we can all recognise. But what about another kind of violence—violence against ourselves? Violence turned inwards? Perhaps I can make the point by connecting two everyday remarks which we often hear. 'I hate myself' and 'He—or she—never has a kind word for anyone'. 'Love your neighbour as yourself' Christ tells us. So we are meant to love our own self. And why not? If none of us is God's enemy, why should we hate our own self? If God does not force us, why should we try to force our own self into the shape we want?

In practice, a decent self-esteem is the platform on which regard for others can be built. It may sound odd to say that self-love is a good thing, when Christian teaching puts so much stress on loving others. But where there is no self-love there is unlikely to be much love for others. As a matter of observation people who despise and dislike themselves usually have little good to say of their neighbours. It is all too easy to get into the habit of belittling everything that other people do, seeing it in the worst possible light, carping and denigrating and generally attempting to drag everyone down to the same contemptible level. Magnanimity, generous respect for others' achievements, stems from a healthy self-respect.

Life is not a competition. God did not invent the rat-race. We do. God made each of us absolutely unique. And he asks each of us to be the unique self he made, not somebody else. The human race is like an enormous orchestra where each player is asked to concentrate on his own instrument and playing in harmony, not in competition, with the rest. It is no good the flute player wanting everyone else to play the flute too. Or resenting the violins, drums and cellos because he cannot make the same noise that they do. God wants each of us to use his own gifts, however humble, and blend in with others, not dominate them or wipe them out. Variety is the hallmark of creation, and how can we value less what the creator plainly values so much.

No use either making war on ourselves. If violence has its limits in putting things right between nations and persons, it certainly has limits in putting matters right within ourselves. The kingdom of heaven is not taken by violence. We have to learn to accept our own nature, especially the dark side of our good qualities. Ferocious attacks on our own weaknesses may drive out one devil but leave room for seven more to enter. It is like weeding. If you just clear the ground and then do nothing with it, the weeds are quickly back. Better to sow and nurture good healthy plants which leave no space for the weeds to grow.

You remember those words in Hamlet. 'We do it violence being so majestical'. Our own nature is majestical. God's own most precious creation, in which he himself shared by coming among us as one of ourselves. We can prize ourselves because God does. We can prize others because he loves them equally. And we can praise, respect and delight in our neighbour's abilities and achievements because we are not in competition in the eyes of God.

A BAD CASE OF BLASPHEMY

We seven-year-olds of St Hengist's, Darlington, woke up to blasphemy as if to an outbreak of war. Indeed, as the real war had been sputtering along for at least twelve months without an audible shot or the thud of a bomb, it threatened more immediate danger. The danger walked and talked and had limitless power. She had only to open the classroom door and you could hear a pin drop. She had only to stand on the edge of the pavement and motorcars gave way to her and their drivers raised their hats. If she so much as looked up at the sky, it was thought, even the German bombers would turn back.

"She" was the headmistress, Sister Matilda, a Sister of (qualified) Charity. She could also, thank heavens, sometimes be a sister of mercy, but on this particular Monday morning her quality of mercy was visibly strained. She looked grim. Worse, her sleeves were rolled up, a certain sign of trouble to come, like a red flag on the beach or an air-raid warning.

Something terrible, she said, had happened. Something so terrible she could not deal with the matter herself. Sharp intakes of breath. Dread thickened the schoolroom smell of boiled milk and putty. What prodigious awfulness could it be that lay beyond the infinite powers of Sister Matilda? Something worse than not putting up your hand in time to leave the room? Something worse than writing a rude word on the school wall? Something even worse than not handing in your dinner money or playing truant? Were all guilty or only one?

The suspense was not protracted. A certain boy, said Sister Matilda, a certain boy had been overheard, overheard by a teacher, saying something truly terrible, something she could not bring herself to repeat, at the school Benediction last Friday evening before the school broke up for the weekend. All heads turned, gingerly, to stare at Robbie Minto. If a certain boy had been stirring up trouble, it was bound to be Robbie Minto. It always was.

Robbie Minto was lean and unsmiling, trained to fight, so rumour went, by two old pugs on the hard edge of town. He prowled the small school yard like a timberwolf, breaking up innocent games of football or marbles, intruding on philosophical conversations about life on other planets or how soon the war would end, and looking for someone to hit. Among his scarred and bleeding victims he had no friends. The class perked up. Perhaps this was not going to turn out too badly after all.

To deal with the unmentionable crime, Sister Matilda went on, she was, for the first time ever, calling in the Canon. No doubt he would scarcely believe what had happened, no doubt he would be shocked as never before in his life. But he would know what to do. She would be back with him later in the morning. And with that she departed. The class phewed with relief and the world turned right side up again.

The Canon being wheeled in offstage was every good Catholic's beau ideal of that distinguished species. He was old, he had white hair, innocent blue eyes, a ruddy complexion, and a respectable, but not gross, embonpoint. He smiled much and spoke little, which gave him an aura of goodness and wisdom. When he preached on the Sunday gospel it was as if he had been an eye-witness, along with the other apostles. He spoke solemnly, with a tremor in his northern voice, which warned that holy things were never to be taken lightly. The Canon was just the man for Robbie Minto.

When Sister Matilda ushered him in as if he were the Holy Father, he was wearing his confession cloak, which together with his flashes of red piping added to his grandeur. "Stand up, Robbie Minto", ordered Sister Matilda without preliminaries. Robbie slowly rose to his feet. "This boy, Canon", she continued, "this boy was heard at Benediction saying something truly dreadful, which I cannot bring myself to repeat. Robbie Minto, tell the Canon what it was you said about the monstrance at Friday's Benediction". Robbie hesitated, drawing back from vain repetitions. "Now then, Robbie", Sister commanded, "tell the Canon what you said." "I said," Robbie uttered in a deadpan voice, "what do you think you'd get for that in a pawnshop?"

The class hid their heads in their hands. The lights dimmed. The Canon drew out his handkerchief, blew loudly and played for time. "Dear me", he said. "You know that was a terrible thing to say,

Robbie?" Robbie nodded. "And you won't do it again?" Robbie nodded a second time. "That's a good boy", said the Canon. "Good-morning, children." And he turned to leave. Sister Matilda looked perplexed. She had called up an artillery barrage and the guns had fired blanks. Another man had proved himself a broken reed. But she hungered for justice and was not without resource. "See me at the end of class, Robbie", she volleyed before she left. The class almost applauded. They at least knew blasphemy when they heard it, and that blasphemers merited vengeance. Especially when the blasphemer was Robbie.

HOME THOUGHTS

Saddling parents with responsibility for everything their children get up to seems to me a clear example of a legal fiction. Were Joseph and Mary irresponsible when the child Jesus lost himself in the Temple? Were Shakespeare's parents to blame when he was up before the beaks for deer-poaching? Even in simpler times parents must have had a hard time keeping track of their children. And the invention of the bicycle has made it virtually impossible. Children are naturally free-range and there must be something wrong with a notion of parental responsibility which would shut them in a broiler house. To cherish, feed, clothe, warm, educate, and instruct by example, yes; but how far further do parental responsibilities really stretch?

I am similarly dubious about the notion of families in which parents and children open their hearts to each other without inhibition. Is this, has it ever been, either right or desirable? Or are there matters on which a natural reticence, even a natural wariness, quite properly prevails? In reality, even in the best-regulated and harmonious families there falls a period when parents and children lapse into cold war. The adolescents wonder what evil planetary conjunction dispensed them such a gruesome pair of wrinklies; and parents search their consciences to know why they deserved such repulsive offspring instead of the nice, well-mannered children they see in church on Sundays. Happily the moment arrives when the children look at other children's parents and decide perhaps that they have not had such a bad deal after all. Meantime the chances for earnest discussions on the meaning of life and in-depth, interpersonal relationships are not high.

Again, it does not strike me as surprising or deplorable that both parents and children will have matters which they will neither wish to reveal to, nor know about, each other. Most societies seem to have recognised a role for neutral third parties, wise women, witch-doctors, dutch uncles, tolerant grannies, and nowadays priests, doctors and social workers, in fielding confidences that might cause unnatural strains within the family circle. True, my own generation were brought up in a state of cateleptic innocence, in a world where all conceptions were immaculate, and if asked leading questions parents were likely to answer stonily that there would be no jam tarts for tea. And the sometimes disturbing consequences have been amply chronicled. But the supposition that total openness is the only alternative to total secrecy is surely somewhat large. I am not at all sure that either parents or children have the duty to reveal all, or the right to know all, even if from time to time, for both parties, some rude shocks result. The only absolute certainty is that whatever they do, parents will get it in the neck and feel they deserve to.

FEELING WORTHLESS

A good deal has been written in recent years on the kind of social problem which can be photographed: bad housing, hunger, handicapped children. Rather less has been said about invisible states of mind which in fact amount to a social problem because they are so widespread and because their effect is to damage the quality of the society we live in. One of these is self-contempt or, to put it another way, a sense of worthlessness.

Like every Catholic, I have heard any number of sermons and exhortations on being humble. Obviously humility can be a strong, appealing virtue, when it means being aware of all that we do not know, and all that have not experienced, and how easily we can make mistakes.

To be humble is to be like the humus, the earth that absorbs the sunlight and rain and stores them until they can feed the seed that is sown in it. But sometimes what the sermons are talking about is a caricature of humility. They simply want us to do without question what others have told us to do without reason. But the man who is passive, unquestioning, uncritical, without a spark of rebellion, is not humble: he is wet, a wimp.

However much damage pride does, lack of pride does just as much. A man who thinks he knows all the answers, that he is lord of all he surveys, that he has a unique built-in guidance system which enables him to avoid all human errors, is a kind of rogue elephant, an active danger to other people as well as himself. But the man who has no respect for himself, no confidence in his abilities, no assurance that other people have any affection or regard for him, is dangerous in a negative way. He is a walking zero. He just is not there when he is wanted or needed. And the world is poorer because the qualities he has, and which could have enriched society, never come to light. The work that does not get done because of strikes is nothing compared with what does not get done because of the number of people who are paralysed by the helpless feeling that they are utterly useless.

There are few sensations which are so debilitating and few so difficult to relieve. Yet almost everybody has a few twinges from time to time. In the Confiteor we express sorrow for 'the things we have failed to do'. It is more than likely that most of these things were not done because we could not believe sufficiently in our capacity to do them.

Man can over-reach himself through pride and fall flat on his face, but he can just as easily under-reach himself and never discover his true ability. Better that, as Browning said, 'a man's reach should exceed his grasp' than that he should not reach far enough.

Things go wrong in the world, we are told, because of man's pride. Personally I believe that men are not proud enough. The real damage is done by those with too little respect for their own humanity, their own individuality, their own gifts and talents. They do not respect the world around them, or their fellow men, because they do not respect themselves. It is the wrong kind of humility which allows the proud to get away with it.

There are dozens of ways of being a drop-out which have nothing to do with being a hippy. It does not require a beard and a kaftan to stop playing any active or creative role in life. Behind featureless faces and square, unremarkable clothes there are plenty of 'burnt-out cases', people in whom the spring has snapped, self-respect drained away, ambition and curiosity dried up.

There is the mother who finds herself spending more and more time staring into space with the empty feeling that she has failed her husband and children in some indefinable way; the husband who moves like a ghost in his own house, afraid that nothing he says will ever be taken seriously; the girl who sits hopelessly by the phone longing for a call that will tell her she is thought of and needed; the young man who is surrounded by contemporaries who seem sharp, assured, and to know exactly what they want, whereas he feels gauche and ineffectual.

Then there is the priest who invents reasons for dodging his parishioners because he feels he has none of the learning, understanding or social gifts which would enable him to be of use; there is the businessman who eats, drinks and sleeps profit and loss because he dare not face himself. All in their way are suffering from the same disease as the hippy who sits in the park stoned out of his mind.

The sense of emptiness, of loneliness, of being a nonentity, of an aching void at the centre of one's being, cuts across ages, occupations and social classes with the cold dispassion of death.

Feeling worthless is a terrible disease because it creates the conditions which turn fantasy into fact. The sense of being a social pariah, useless and hopeless, can begin as a figment of imagination but end as an accepted reality. The boy who lacks assurance soon creates an antimagnetic field around him and produces exactly the effect he painfully wished to avoid. The girl who feels unattractive and unloved isolates herself by her own diffidence and makes her nightmare come true.

A certain deftness and self-confidence are necessary in personal relationships, just as attractive and necessary as they are in ballet, painting or carpentry. When they are lacking, people shy away, as they shy away from a drunk—and for the same reasons.

A sense of worthlessness is a moral cancer which it is difficult to cure once it has taken root. But at least we can help in building up resistance to it. So often individuals and institutions claim to be waging a war on pride, when in fact they are simply stamping on the already half-defeated.

Schools for example are so quick to snuff out 'conceit', 'complacency', 'over-confidence' that what they actually snuff out is essential self-respect. And often it seems that individuals are trying to prove their intelligence by expert analysis of their friends' defects, when it would show greater intelligence to single out their merits.

We could all do so much by learning to encourage, to praise, to pick out good points instead of bad.

There are other kinds of malnutrition than hunger for bread. All of us know how we need affection, encouragement and praise. Yet we are so slow to give it. And there is no more woeful person than the one who is starved of love, and starved of praise.

If a Martian visited earth to find out what human beings value in each other by studying our books, films, advertisements and conversation, he would probably settle on good looks, plenty of money, social status, professional success and power over other people. Our whole society is geared to making these the criteria of personal worth.

Of course if we actually thought about it we would say this was wrong. None of us likes being loved and admired for what we own, or what we wear, where we live or what we do. We want to be loved for our own self, no matter how poor a self it seems to be. But in the society to which we belong, and which we help to make, it is hardly those who are honest but poor, kind but ugly, hard-working but powerless, who receive most deference and attention.

And yet to base self-esteem on the wrong things means that we are doomed to disappointment. Good looks fade, and few have them to start with. Most people can never hope to be rich, famous or influential. In every walk of life it gets narrower towards the top; there are always more majors than ever will be colonels, and success may depend as much on luck as on ability. If we think that our value depends on riches and beauty, failure is written into the script. If it does, most of the human race are to be looked down on as worthless. If it does, then I only have to look into the mirror, empty my pockets or ring up the local council to make a complaint, and I will feel at once that I am worthless. Saddest of all, only a few are likely to know the ideal human love which bolsters confidence and brings contentment. It is an eerie feeling to look up at the night sky and realise that some of the stars we are looking at no longer exist. The light still reaches us but there is no substance behind it; the star died long ago. When the advertisements tell us to hitch our wagon to this star or that, beauty or power or riches, we need to ask whether these are not dead stars too, all shimmer and no substance. It takes a cool head and a deep faith to resist this propaganda and remind ourselves that salvation is for all, and every man the object of God's love.

Christ did not come for those who are all right, but for those who are all wrong. The rheumy tramp and the painted lady have exactly the same reason to prize themselves, that for love of each God became man, was crucified and rose again, and that each, through Christ, can call God Father. Through the eyes of society most of us are worthless: through the eyes of God, not one.

A mediocre cricketer usually plays his strokes with an air of hurried improvisation. He looks under pressure. A great batsman, on the other hand, bats with an air of unhurried calm and spaciousness. In our relationship with God we need this sense of spaciousness, of time to play our strokes so to speak, and one of the worst effects of feeling worthless is to deprive us precisely of this. Every second seems at once both hopeless and critical, every choice to be hurried yet loaded with doom.

The answer lies in grasping that God's love is particular, personal and for everybody; and that it is offered to us not as we could be but as we are. The trouble is that this oldest of Christian truths can seem extremely unreal. Sometimes God's love can seem like a volcano among remote mountains, burning away without heating anybody. And from our side it sometimes seems inconceivable that any individual can be worth noticing, never mind loving. To stand in a busy street and watch the cataract of humanity flooding by is to be oppressed by the apparent insignificance of the individual. So many anonymous faces, so many personalities we shall never know, with all their particular relatives and friends, their jqbs, their experiences, their ideals, hopes and sufferings. To talk of individual value seems a mockery among so many people. What on earth can it mean to talk of God loving each of us?

Against this feeling stand the Gospels, the Letters of St Paul and the experience of countless saints, both known and unknown. One of the most striking lines in the New Testament is Paul's astonished exclamation: Christ loves *me,* Christ died for *me.* He of course had heard Christ calling him by his own name but—'blessed are those who have not seen and have believed'. Continually in the Gospels we see Christ's concern for the individual breaking through. He calls his apostles individually, heals the sick and the sinners not in clusters but as far as possible one by one. It is quite surprising how vividly minor characters stand out: the paralytic and the tenth leper, the centurion, the widow of Naim, Mary Magdalen and Zacchaeus. They are only pencilled in, but precisely defined.

This impression of particular value is reinforced by Our Lord's words. In the parable of the lost sheep, the story of the prodigal son, the statement that not a hair falls from our heads without our heavenly Father noticing, he dramatises the importance of each individual not because of their merits or importance but because of their humanity. He has come, he tells us, not for the just but for sinners. It is the poor, not the rich, who are to have the gospel preached to them. And he claims to have come that all, not just a chosen few, may be saved.

God is concerned with communities but not with mobs. Every man, woman and child counts. It is no compensation for parents who have lost a child to know they still have several left. It is no consolation to God our Father that most are saved, if one is lost. Human love may be denied us, but God's at least is not confined to deserving causes.

AN EXCHANGE OF GIFTS

My late revered uncle, whose instincts were as wise as time, had a soft spot for tramps. To the looming Victorian presbytery, opposite Newcastle bus station and sandwiched between the central fire and police stations, which was for a quarter of a century his own and many others' unlikely hearth, at least a score turned up daily for a bed, clothing, food, or the price of a drink. None was ever turned away. That in itself is remarkable. There are many such priests and presbyteries up and down the land where the unjustified poor find help, with no questions asked.

More remarkable was the respect and even admiration in which he held the tramps. They were never, as sometimes appears, merely instruments on which the godly might play their tunes. Without sentiment, he perceived some smack of virtue in their lonely independence and secretly enjoyed the fact that they fouled up the cradle-to-grave welfare system beloved of social technicians who want a society that runs like a clean machine. The tramps were certainly not clean.

But he perceived something more important still. Some years ago he decided to give the tramps a Christmas party. A small expeditionary force turned up, casting about warily for the strings they were sure must be attached; free tracts on indulgences, green scapulars, pictures of the Little Flower, even the dreaded pledge. There were none, and in later years, reassured by their scouts, the main army arrived and yearly swelled in numbers. By trial and error a few ground rules were established. No prettification—tablecloths, flowers on the table and the like. No outsiders. Above all, no photographs.

On one occasion I happened to be staying at the presbytery just after Christmas, when the tramps party was held. It was a bleak winter, and deep snow covered the churchyard and the street outside. When the feasting and carolling were done, and the tramps were departing, my uncle suddenly announced that he would be grateful for a few volunteers to help clear away the snow the following morning. Oaths and promises rang through the frosty air. I, poor sophisticate, retired thinking my own cynical thoughts, and, if truth be told, mildly embarrassed. Next morning, much to my surprise, not one, not three or four, but a dozen tramps stood on the doorstep awaiting orders. Extra brushes and shovels were hastily commandeered from our civic neighbours. Off to work went the tramps, digging and heaving and scraping and brushing till, an hour later, both yard and street were as clean as a bone; all, that is, except for a length of pavement outside the police station.

One by one the tramps handed in their tools and departed, until only two were left. "Just a moment," said my uncle, "I've a suitcase here full of copper from the Christmas collections. It's a bit on the heavy side. Would you take it up to the bank and I'll meet you there in twenty minutes." "Aye, Father. Certainly, Father." And picking up the suitcase like a coffin the two tramps set off up the street and disappeared from view. When the door was closed I turned to my uncle and asked, brimful of incredulity, "What's to stop them nipping round the next corner and disappearing with it?" "Nothing," he said, "but they won't. They'll be telling the story for a month. 'Father told us to go to the bank with this great big suitcase full of money.' They'll be as pleased as Punch." Sure enough, when we got to the bank the tramps were waiting patiently, their faces set with a heavy sense of responsibility, every line of their bodies warning passers-by to keep their distance.

Those tramps come back to mind every time I think of the shepherds and the wise men. There they kneel in a thousand Christmas cribs, their faces full of wonderment at the birth of Christ; the wise and the simple, the rich and the poor, side by side. And in their hands, lambs and gold and frankincense and myrrh. In the manger God's most extraordinary gift to mankind, Himself, revealed in the face of a child. The infinite placed within reach, and surrounded by finite men. The All-Wise, the All-Powerful, the God who has Everything, making Himself known to the frail and foolish. Yet they offer, and He accepts, their gifts. What divine delicacy it is that spares mankind the humiliation of feeling it has nothing to offer. The giving is not one-way. Man's own dignity is saved, and God's gift of Himself becomes acceptable, because the gifts of our representatives at Bethlehem are found acceptable. It is a lesson and a warning to all who wish to do good to others. Those who care for the poor, the sick and the handicapped. Those who welcome the migrant and visit the prisons. Those who set out with evangelical fervour to take the Gospel or technology to foreign lands. Even for goverments as they sit at the conference table planning the rich countries' aid and development schemes for the poor. There will be no gratitude and no reconciliation if the giving is all one-way. To be perpetually on the receiving end of even kindly-meant benevolence is both degrading and demoralising. It accounts for much bitterness and tension between individuals and between nations. It is blessed to give, but twice blessed is he who is not too high-and-mighty to receive in return. To ask favours of the poor does more for their dignity than a thousand hand-outs. Even the poorest feel the need to give. The Second Shepherds' Play of the Towneley Cycle hits off the instinct both comically and beautifully:

My hart wolde blede
To se Thee sitt here in so poore wede,
With no pennis.
Haill! Put furth thy dall! (hand)
I bring Thee bot a ball:
Have and play Thee withall,
And go to the tenis.

God knew a thing or two when he accompanied the birth of his Son
with an exchange of gifts.

THE LOT OF THE UNEMPLOYED

Cardinal Joseph Bernardin, of Chicago has spoken of the
"astonishingly low self-image" which families in poverty have of
themselves. "Many poor persons are convinced of their inability to
acquire basic skills needed to contribute to society." His statement
has a much wider reference than the poor in the United States, to
whom he was referring. Perhaps the worst effect of unemloyment is
the psychological damage it does to those who are out of work in
societies where being in work is an official stamp of self-approval
as well as of social respect. In addition, being in work is the first
item on the invisible identity card we all carry. "What do you do?"
is, often irritatingly, the first question we ask and are asked when
we talk to strangers. To answer "I say my prayers, love my wife,
cherish my children, practise honesty, and tend my garden" may all
be true and more important in the sight of God as well, perhaps, as
being a better clue to character, but in ordinary conversation it
would be dismissed as a roundabout way of answering "nothing."
And "nothing" is the word that dare not be spoken. Not, anyway,
in a society where, like a grim parody of Marxism, those who work
hardest are thought to be richest in merit, and those who work least
to be good-for-nothings or scroungers. It may be unfair, since
"having a job" is increasingly a matter of luck as well as of will, initiative and qualification; it may be irrational, since those who have
jobs may be doing work which results in all kinds of mischief.
Faces that light up with interest at the farmer or the book-maker
describing his trade cloud over when the jobless tells his troubles:
he has tried for a hundred jobs and failed in all; he cannot afford to
travel all over the country seeking employment; he cannot bear
forcing his wife and children to leave their friends, relatives and
familiar surroundings; he has been trained for the wrong type of
work; he has no strings to pull; joblessness itself becomes an almost

insurmountable obstacle to getting a job. Few have an ear for these litanies of pain. If the poor have a low self-image, being out of work, or in work precariously and for brief spells only, is in itself sufficient reason. Daily they are made to feel useless and unwanted, and the corroding effect of that experience can easily tarnish relationships even within the family circle.

Unemployment is not, however, the only experience common to the poor which undermines confidence. There is also the difficulty of getting a hearing on matters which vitally affect their lives, when the language, style and conventions of public discourse are all unfamiliar, and frequently daunting. In many third world countries this has been clearly recognised by the community groups springing up in slums and peasant villages. They see that men and women who are used to being treated as no more than hewers of wood and drawers of water must have their confidence patiently built up and be taught appropriate techniques before they can get their views across to officials with force and conviction. But as the cardinal indicates, there are many people in affluent societies who also feel "shut-out," who also take it for granted that they will not be heard, and who are equally ill at ease when their surroundings, the conventions, and the language employed are all outside their experience. It is often noticed that in local politics, voluntary organisations, pressure groups, advisory councils and public discussions the middle-classes play a predominant part; and it is sometimes assumed that this is because they have the necessary money and leisure, as well as a keen sense of self-interest. But at least as important a reason is that the poor feel that to take part in these matters they must enter a foreign country. The vocabulary, the tone, the pace of discussion, inhibit a large proportion of the population from taking part. They are not less wise. They are not necessarily less well-informed. They are at sea. We need to recognise that the style of public discourse and its conventions have been developed into an art form over a long period of time. They encourage sweet reason, patient listening, giving the other side a chance to speak, couching even hard sayings in terms designed not to insult or offend, sticking to the point. But many people have never had the chance to learn these airs and graces, valuable though they are and a distillation of much bitter experience. For those accustomed to a more rambling, repetitive, and astringent style, and whose vocabulary is more limited, breaking into a different kind of conversation is as hard as mastering some technical skill. The skills the poor need to acquire go beyond the learning of a trade. First above all is the skill to make themselves heard. "We are the people of this land, and we have not spoken yet.'' Not, I think, because they have nothing to say, or because they have no will to say it. But because public discourse has rules, and only a minority know them.

THE EXPERIENCE OF POVERTY

It would be comforting to think that sight of the poor always inspires pity and an urge to ride to the rescue. In fact, I believe, our attitudes are extremely complex, ranging from the judgement that the poor are not only deprived but blameworthy to the romanticising of their condition as precious in the sight of God. The one common feature is that each in some fashion diminishes our own responsibility and offers an excuse for inaction.

An inkling of these complex feelings came to me when very young. My first brush with real poverty was like stepping into a page of Dickens. I must have been about nine years old, and while out walking one evening in a northern town where I was visiting relatives, met a curate from the local parish church. He asked if I would take a message to an old lady on the other side of town to say he would be bringing her communion the following morning. The area was unfamiliar and the address proved to be a small courtyard off a narrow lane. The room I entered was dark, damp and almost unfurnished. The stench was appalling. The old lady, sitting by an empty grate, was surly and suspicious. Two children, dirty and ragged, and about my own age, stared ferociously out of the gloom. I delivered my message and bolted. And my reaction to this disconcerting scene, I regret to say, was not pity but fear. As for my relatives, when I told my adventure, their reaction was that the curate had no business sending me to such a place.

I received a second lesson some three years later, after we had moved to London. One afternoon I went to play with a friend from school. While we were absorbed in some game or other on the sitting-room floor, I gradually became aware that the adults talking over our heads were heatedly denouncing the whole tribe of coalminers. Though it was wartime there had been rumours of a strike and not unreasonably this was regarded as distinctly unpatriotic. But, less reasonably, the gist of their remarks was that miners were now paid like pirates and living in clover. Fresh from County Durham, I quickly concluded that little though I knew about miners it was prodigiously more than they did. Uninvited, I chipped in to restore the balance of reality. After a few at first startled, then angry, exchanges. I was told I was being precocious and impertinent and was escorted from the room.

75

Here again—I sensed that the root of this evident reluctance to face unpalatable facts about the pay and conditions of miners was fear. It was less threatening to look for reassurance in comforting myths than to face the implications of what just possibly might be a justified grievance.

Anecdotes apart, these instincts, to fear the poor, to blame them for their sorry state, to give them a wide berth, are common. The poor are an awful warning of what could be. They inhabit a gulf along the edge of which all of us walk. There, we say, but for the grace of God and my own diligence, go I. The poor—and they exist—who are so by their own fault do not disturb our ordered universe of cause and effect. The disturbing poor are those who are undeserving victims of circumstance or of decisions and arrangements which might have been different. It is they who shake our sense of security, make the ground wobble under our feet, because they make life look like a lottery in which my own number may turn up no matter what means I take to prevent it. That, rather than unwelcome claims they may invite upon the pocket, is, I surmise, what sparks aggressive feelings towards the poor.

At the opposite end of the spectrum a pious romanticising of the poor can have similar practical effects. Perhaps less rarely heard than it used to be, the view still steals into religious exhortations that to be poor is to be blessed; that the poor are happier, nobler, less anxious, more open-hearted, than those who labour under the disability of money and possessions. Sometimes, of course, it is so. The very poor can and do sometimes rise to heights of heroism in terrible conditions. But sometimes they behave quite otherwise and understandably turn bitter and vicious. Certainly the state of poverty cannot be commended without qualification as a sure road to sanctity. Voluntary poverty may purify the spirit; but involuntary poverty is a horse of a different colour and to equate the two is to turn an affliction into a charism. In practice its distressing consequence can be, like fearing and blaming them, to distance ourselves from the poor; to praise and patronise them instead of offering relief. Here too, in a subtler way, our own responsibility is diminished, and the poor are required to fend for themselves. The truth is that the poor are our responsibility, an individual and collective responsibility, and that alleviating poverty, with all its crippling effects on human development, a Christian duty. And if we find ourselves shying from it, it is useful to delve for the reasons.

THE ONE AND THE MANY

There was once a nun who, when she was well into her sixties, took up swimming. From swimming she progressed to diving and for a number of years thereafter happily water-sported throughout the summer months. But when she reached the age of 75 and showed no sign of diminishing enthusiasm her community began to feel tremors of alarm. It seemed to them unlikely that so many sharp blows to her venerable head could be doing her much good and they made this collective view known to their mother superior. She, with that blend of solicitude and judiciousness which so becomes mother superiors, called in the diver and addressed her thus: "Imprudentia", she said, "we are all delighted that you enjoy swimming so much; but your sisters feel — and I have to agree with them — that at your age diving is unwise. Perhaps, don't you think, the time has come to give it up?" The nun had been in religion long enough to know when a polite question was slamming down the lid. With a resigned gesture, a crestfallen look, and in the tones of someone who has just dropped her keys down a drain, she replied "Oh, paradise lost!"

This edifying tale supplies at least one answer to another ageing lady I used to know who had a different obsession. It was the injustice, as she saw it, of having to pay rates for the building of a neighbourhood swimming-pool, when, as she declared, she "would never be using it". In the light of the nun's story one might have answered, "Well, you never know", though no doubt she would have considered this facetious.

An alternative, *ad feminam,* answer might have been, and probably was, that it could be worth a modest contribution to raise the chances that the local young people were disporting themselves in the swimming-pool rather than knocking old ladies over the head. But a third and fuller answer, once the buzzing of a bee in the bonnet had diminished, should have been that we are all part of a human community and making it a better community goes beyond paying only for those improvements of direct benefit to ourselves. It is better to be part of a community which has libraries even if we do not read, and parks even if we cannot walk, and schools even if we are into middle age, and fire engines even if our house never catches fire, because the more civilised and fulfilled and competent and secure the people we live among, the more pleasant our life, however indirectly, is likely to be. And indeed the eventide homes we objected to paying for when young and limber may be just what we are looking for when we have lost interest in swimming-pools.

Reflection on such matters makes it seem still more absurd to argue that there is no such thing as society but only individuals and families; and that we must all individually get only what we pay for and pay for anything we get. Leaving aside the rather obtrusive exceptions to that line of argument—it is never suggested we should individually arm ourselves with swords and shields rather than collectively with jet fighters—a human community is a palpable thing, palpably more than the sum of its parts, and requiring all sorts of cross-fertilisation and mutual support if the individuals who constitute it are to achieve true personhood.

Both slums without swimming-pools and suburbs whose every household has a private swimming-pool are wastelands of the spirit, where the sense of community, of mutual need and obligation, is corroded. But at least the pool-owners get the chance to swim. As usual it is the poor who suffer most when the sense of community is absent and the "pay or do without" philosophy prevails.

The point was highlighted recently when a local concert of Handel's *Firework Music* and a display of fireworks was advertised. Just the thing, you might say, for a family evening out. But there was a catch. The tickets were £ 12 each. That kind of pricing shuts out millions of people from a whole range of cultural and social advantages and activities as effectively as armed guards and barbed wire. And where community obligation is weakened, the range of cultural goods denied to the poor is bound to grow wider.

That is bad for the individuals concerned, for as Pope John Paul points out, there are more kinds of poverty than the lack of material goods (including swimming-pools), and intellectual and cultural deprivation are high among them; but it is also bad for the community, including its old ladies. A community where large numbers of people have their access to cultural goods blocked off is in worse case than one where there is no chance to swim. It is a formula for promoting bad ideas and bad feelings as well as bad relationships. And the price of that will fall on all, regardless of their ability or willingness to pay.

THE MASS

One morning when I was visiting friends we were celebrating Mass and thinking about its special meaning in Bradford-on-Avon, a town famous for its beauty and antiquity. Like everything beautiful it is individual, unique—of course it has plenty in common with other towns, but there is no mistaking it for somewhere

else. Again its ancient buildings, so many of them dating back to the early Middle Ages, are a living thread of continuity, a constant reminder of the efforts of men and women over centuries past to build a human community on this spot. In both ways it is like the Mass, for every celebration is an individual event fresh as Spring yet each shares much in common with all the Masses being celebrated throughout the world today and every Mass celebrated right back to the first two thousand years ago.

Bradford is a witness in stone to two facts about human life; the fact that everyone wants to be individual and special and to express that sense of difference in the things they make, and the fact that no one can be truly human isolated from others. We have to band together with other people, draw closer to them, and the Mass, I believe, has a bearing on both those facts. It has a meaning for each of us as an individual person and as a community. It is a pity that we have so often talked about 'going to Mass' as if it was a duty, something that really goes against the grain but we do because God, like some vain old War Lord, insists that at least once a week we should all pay him our respects, salute him to acknowledge that he s in charge and keep in his good books. But that cannot be, for 'othing that God has done through his Son, Jesus Christ, is done or his own good. The Mass is not said for God, it is for us, for our 'enefit. So it is these two aspects of the Mass that I want to examine more closely: its meaning for our own full human development, and the growth of community.

When anyone makes something which involves skill and effort, hey want to show it to others. The poet wants to publish his oems, the artist to put his pictures on show, the musician to give a concert. A mother when she has baked a cake does not prick it with a straw to see if it is done then take it out of the oven and straight way throw it into the dustbin. She waits for the family to come in and see them enjoy it and tell her what a marvellous cook she is. But how does anyone express in that kind of way what they have made of themselves as a human being, the meaning of their life, what they live for, what they stand for. Almost everything we do only reveals an aspect of ourselves. If we vote, we express the fact that we are citizens. If we go to a football match we reveal only that we are interested in sport and if we go shopping, we do so in our role as a consumer. On the face of it there seems no way of expressing our whole humanity all at once. But that, I think, is exactly what taking part in the Mass enables us to do. Here in the company of other members of the Christian family, we make a declaration just by being present about the meaning of all that we are, the faith

we live by, the purpose of our life and the value we attach to it. We bring our own meaning to the Mass, and each time it brings new meaning to all that we do and all that we are. At the same time, none of us comes as a complete human being, the finished article so to speak. We all wear a placard round our necks saying 'Work in Progress'. So at the offertory when we offer the simplest basics of human life—food and drink, and ask our Father in heaven to change them into the Body and Blood of his Son, we offer also all our powers of body and mind, our hopes and past experience, our outward activities and inner instincts, our dreams and desires and even our lapses and failures and ask that this basic human stuff should also be transformed, reflect and be suffused by God himself. We offer to the Father all that we are, all that we do, all that we possess and all that we hope to be; and we offer it through his Son, by the power of the Holy Spirit. And the Father, through his Son, who became a man like us, by the gift of his spirit which he left with us, joins in the work of shaping us into fully human beings. He does so by sharing his Divine power and presence and guaranteeing it under the appearance of bread and wine—once again, simple, ordinary human things. So much for the individual at Mass, but as we all realise, if we are to lead a full human life we have to mix with other people. If we cannot talk, share ideas, mix socially, it is like being crippled. One of the worst punishments is to put a man into solitary confinement, or send someone to Coventry. Without human company we shrivel up. Much of our lives is spent getting to know other people better and drawing closer to them, and a great deal is written nowadays about how to build up human communities that can help individuals to lead richer lives and in which each person can find the affection, support and encouragement they need.

The need to make contact with others is shown in all kinds of ways. At one end of the scale there is a brief contact when you catch the eye of a stranger in the street and nod or smile. It is a fleeting moment but there has been some kind of acknowledgement and exchange. Then there is the commuter who, every day, says good morning to the ticket collector. Even though they never get beyond that, after a while they have quite a degree of friendly feeling and understanding; and a bit closer is the kind of contact of two men talking on the terrace at a football match, or two women talking in a queue at the shops. They may never meet again, but just for a while there is a tenuous bond between them. Sometimes that instinct to create links with others is more deliberate. People form groups—they have been to the same school or belonged to the same

regiment; or because they share the same interest like stamp-collecting or bird-watching, or a common cause like helping the homeless or trying to stop a motorway ruining an ancient city. And there are other still closer communities which people deliberately create like religious communities or communes; and there are communities to which we belong whether we like it or not, like our families or our country. But I think we are all aware that our best efforts to create bonds with others and to build communities in which we can thrive, fall short. We sense that there is a deeper union which people crave and which some, just occasionally, are lucky enough to glimpse—a union of perfect peace and concord, of complete openness, of completely understanding and being completely understood, of perfectly loving and being perfectly loved, of being at one in heart, in mind and spirit, of being perfectly in tune with others. It is the difference between community and communion. Man can create communities, but can only go so far; the union beyond that which he senses exists is a gift from outside himself. Lovers sometimes feel it, a mother and child may feel it. Sometimes even a group of people can momentarily feel perfectly in tune with each other. You may have noticed how, during the quiet time after Communion, a deep stillness seems to fall on everybody and seep through them and bind them together, if only for a few moments; and just for a moment we have an inkling of how the world might be if such peace stretched from pole to pole and the whole human family were united like that in their depths each one with every other, and all one with each other.

Well, the perfect timeless, unrepeatable sacrifice of Christ to which we are admitted at every Eucharist is the womb of that peace and union—union with God through a treaty of friendship which is everlasting and signed with the heart's blood of Jesus Christ, God, the Son made man for us: communion between all who receive the body of the Lord through which flow the life, the energy, the peace of God himself into our frozen hearts and blinkered minds. Bonded with Christ in the Eucharist, we are bonded with each other, not on the surface through words, looks, gestures, by physical contact or travelling from place to place, but in the very depths of our being; through the sacrifice of Christ on Calvary, making peace between God and man, the gift of Communion is offered to us. There can be peace between man and man, and through us if we are open to this gift, God can in the words of St Athanasius draw together the things in the air with those on earth, and those in heaven with those in the air and combine the whole with the parts, linking them by his command and will, thus producing in beauty and harmony a single world and a single order within it.

THE ALTERNATIVE LIFE

Many years ago I came by accident on the Goan Mass at Westminster Cathedral in honour of St Francis Xavier. The cathedral was thronged with Goans now settled in this country, and their choir and orchestra, assembled *ad hoc* for the occasion, sang and played with fine control and delicacy of feeling. And if they felt they were called upon to sing the songs of Sion in a strange land they gave no sign of it, for on every side their smiles and greeting lit up a wet December night.

It seemed so strange, as the preacher told again the story of Francis Xavier, to think how four centuries ago Europe sent the great apostle to the Indies, and how here in the heart of London their descendants were gathered to celebrate the gift of faith, returning, in Helen Prescott's phrase, "like argosies deep-laden." This, if any, is the alternative life, unremarked by newspapers or bulletins, the tide of faith that ebbs and flows mysteriously across the earth and down the centuries, sometimes given, sometimes received, but always and everywhere making a fertile field for hope and for the children of hope, friendship, compassion and delight. Friendship which makes from scattered individuals a wood that even the fiercest storm cannot blow down: compassion which solaces the injured and breaks the vicious circle of violence and revenge: and delight which faith can find in even the most barren places of the earth and the lowest depths of the spirit. These are the capacities which help us ride the waves of despair, no virtues are more Christian, and wherever the Christian faith takes root in the soul they thrive. At a time when bitter enmities, harsh exploitation and sour cynicism tear the human race apart, they are the best that Christian faith has to offer: and perhaps in Europe they will only be renewed when Christian missionaries carry them to us as we once carried them to others.

There is another thought. At any given time the hard men and the cunning seem to have the best of it. The callous, the ambitious, the greedy, over and over again direct the world's courses. But how many of them could centuries after their death gather men of a different colour from a different continent to venerate their memory as Francis Xavier gathered these Goans. The statesmen, the generals and the men of affairs may rule the roost for a handful of years but it is the mystics and the poets and the men of luminous, practical faith who outlast time and who father generations of disciples to pay them willing affectionate honour without the threat of the sword or the bait of gold. Hardly a score of tyrants are remembered, and none loved, against the thousands of saints who still find a corner in the human heart, and not a dozen torturers against the memory of countless of their victims whose lives are recorded in detail. Not only recorded but cherished, venerated, and a cause of festivity.

Like an oyster, the human race secretes the memory of the good, though the fact is so familiar that it ceases to astonish. It is those who have preached love, forgiveness, unselfishness, the supremacy of the spirit, who draw men to worship, not those who on earth have built up empires and held the power of life and death. And in the heroes it chooses to remember, the God who under different forms it worships, mankind gives away its own deepest belief about the meaning and purpose of life and the way that life is to be lived. And just as that belief is so often obscured by the drama of public events, so many of them cruel and tragic, so too is its daily practice. The friendly greetings, the words of encouragement and sympathy, the small acts of kindness which people exchange a thousand times a day, and most of all in times of trouble, are a better clue to the spirit of man than the sad public events. The good goes unremarked.

DARLINGTON MAN

When I was growing up, Mr Marley, Mr Dodds and Mr Selby were an *awful* trinity in every neighbourhood child's pattern of days, topping in importance even the small house whose front window was crammed with steaming homemade bread, and jam and lemon-curd tarts.

Mr Marley had a wall-eye—or was it glass?—which gave him 360° vision, a necessary knack for he sold comics and every kind of marble under the sun. The marbles gave us healthy exercise pursuing them along the sooty and too frequently soaking-wet pavements. The comics stirred our hearts to bursting with patriotic sentiments and opened up the world of foreign affairs.

Mr Dodds was a quiet, grey grocer who every Friday, as regular as clockwork, sent all life's necessities to my home in a large cardboard box. But his claim to immortality was his lemonade, with his Tizer a close runner-up. Keeping up the quality of these products must have been a burden for him, for he never smiled, but he did give a ha'penny back on returned bottles.

It was Mr Selby in his barber shop who was the greatest of the three. He was a small sparrow of a man, of boundless benevolence and shiny black hair glued from forehead to nape. He knew everything, and was generous with his knowledge. Snip-snip he would go, as unhurried old men puffed on their Woodbines and small boys tried to sneak a look at Jane of the the *Daily Mirror.* Snip-snip. And out would tumble a non-stop commentary on the conduct of the war (we were losing), the private lives of filmstars, the crookedness of local councillors, the history of the town, and the current state of hostilities between Methodists, Catholics and Quakers who made up most of the population with a salting of Anglicans to keep up the tone and see fair play. Nowadays he would have been snapped up for *Any Questions?* or be writing a column in a weekly journal "Mr Selby warns the Chancellor: sixpence too much for short back and sides."

In our small world he was very up to date. There were then plenty of people in Darlington for whom Mr Gladstone's views on Home Rule were still a live issue, and the Great War merely an English plot for distracting attention from the Irish question. Mr Selby had moved on. He knew that Mr Churchill was a good leader in war but a bad leader in peace. He knew that after the war Mr Churchill would be "rejected by the electorate," his very words, and Labour sweep to victory. He knew that Britain would become an American colony, and rationing continue till we were all ready for our graves. He knew that the Quakers, the town football team, would never get out of the Fourth Division because the directors would not be able to afford the travelling expenses if they did. He knew, in short, all there was to know, and we hung on every word, while every now and again an intrepid old man would take his Woodbine out of his mouth long enough to interject "Yer right, Jack" before the flood rolled on.

Mr Selby was better than the *Northern Echo,* then still awaiting the full revelation of its inner glory by Mr Harold Evans, and the Pink Un rolled into one. And on party politics he was definitive. Parties, he would say, were like religious sects—all going the same road. Labour was for the working man. The Conservatives were gentlemen and born to rule, but they did not know much about life. But neither he would sum up, cocking at an angle whichever head he was trimming, teasing out a stray hair with his comb and lopping it off, neither "has ever done owt for Darlington"; and each old man, as he stood up at the end of his haircut to have his shoulders brushed and be asked *sotto voce* whether there was anything else he wanted, would intone: "Yer right Jack, politicians are all daft."

THE AFTERNOON OF LIFE

"Will you take part," said the voice on the telephone, "in a seminar on Spirituality for the Middle-Aged?" Hah. The secret was out. All those pathetic attempts to run upstairs two at a time, all that careful combing of hair over the shiny bits, all that laboured Swedish drill performed by the dawn's early light; all wasted, all defences blown. To be middle-aged in the privacy of one's mind is bad enough; to be *officially* docketed as middle-aged—what gall, what wormwood. "Yes," I said, meekly.

And so we arrived, lured by Jesuit persuasiveness and Notre Dame hospitality, with half-a-dozen other listed historic couples, at a dour Edwardian pile in the middle of Clapham Common, there to be waited on in our decrepitude by a number of far from decrepit young nuns, and to reflect on our condition. We were joined by two Jesuits, both so spiritual they could have passed through cheesecloth without disturbing the mesh, one Jungian Redemptorist from Scotland, and one Freudian Redemptorist from Ireland, set to pick us apart and put us together again before we must settle for the wheelchair and the ear-trumpet.

Certainly the opening session was enough to scare the hide off less battle-scarred veterans. Would we please, asked the director, each explain our present state of mind and soul and how we had reached it? Later we would be enriched with much contemporary research about the afternoon of life, and in the light of it take counsel together about our future prospects, especially those of the spirit.

Our first collective decision, typically spirited, was to cast aside all talk of a crisis of middle-age. We were full of hope, our eyes fixed on the sunlit uplands of old age, and the even sunnier pastures of paradise beyond. So away with the heart-sighs and heart-searchings of mere youth, and down to the positive lessons of experience, the checking over of equipment already well-tested on life's battlefield, and realistic planning of the penultimate stage of our earthly expedition.

What, then, came out of it? First, we had all come, we discovered, despite hard times and painful interludes, to a deep conviction that the God we intuit, sometimes glimpse, argue and wrestle with, adore, invoke and protest against, is truly loving and benevolent; and this not from blind faith in some preached dogma but as an unassailable truth of the heart, a conviction which had built up steadily like a coral reef, not despite but in the very experience of doubt, grief and affliction, as well as of joy and contentments.

Second, we had moved steadily from a welter of poorly coordinated "beliefs," impressions and conjectures, to a few simple, strongly held and closely interwoven convictions which served effectively both for the interpretations of life and as principles of action. Third, we felt a profound urge to bring these essential beliefs into ever sharper focus and the outer active life into close conformity with them. We had passed, we found, not only through the easily impressionable time of youth but through youth's compulsive desire to impress. The key experience of middle age appears to be a paradox—a realistic sense of limitations, a jettisoning of ambitions, inflated self-regard and airy illusions (which might indeed be expected to result in doleful melancholy), but, hand in hand with these, a stirring sense of liberation, a steadier experience of joy, a quiet realisation that "to thine own self be true" is not only a wise human word but the Lord's command. Baptism launches a separate identity into the Christian community, the arena of human life. Our task is to discover, express and complete that identity in all its individual richness and complexity.

Perhaps that sounds complacent. It was not a complacent group but one firmly rooted in the humdrum realities of money, jobs, child-rearing, and personal relations. It may sound pietistic. But along with overall gratitude for having sailed in the barque of Peter went plenty of tales of sea-sickness. It may sound privileged. And true, only the middle-class, middling-prosperous, middle-aged can take time off for bouts of soul-searching; those in other states and walks of life might have brought less reassuring messages from the battlefront. Nonetheless, we all have to play the hand we are dealt, and our circumstances in life are an aspect of the self to which we must be true. Yet the lonely, handicapped, under-privileged, the older and younger, were far from forgotten. The middle-aged are used to headshakings and reproachful mutters, to standing aside sheepishly while pastors and preachers concentrate their fire on the more promising material of youth. A weekend to themselves was not much to ask.

EVANGELISATION A LA RUSSE

I was walking one afternoon through the city of Newcastle with my late uncle, whom persistent readers are already familiar with as the ungovernable parish priest of St Andrew's, Worswick Street, when we were saluted by an elderly and handsome man who stopped briefly to exchange civilities. He was a foreigner, from the accent a Slav, a man of refinement and courtesy, the kind of man who can quote Dostoievsky at the sound of a bell and who makes one confusedly conscious of one's unshone shoes, bagging trousers and uncombed hair. When we had each fired a volley of pleasantries, we made our farewells and went our ways.

"Who was that?" I asked, intrigued. "He supplies me with converts", said my uncle, walking on with an ambiguous smile. I pressed him again, and at last, for once casting off his customary discretion, he told me the following baffling tale.

The gentleman—he was certainly that—was a Count B, a White Russian driven from his home and pursued across Europe by Bolsheviks till he found am improbable but safe haven in Newcastle. By doing a bit of this and that, a notorious faculty of expatriate White Russians in those days, especially the 99 per cent or so claiming to be counts, barons or even first cousins of the Tsar, he kept body and soul together, dividing what leisure time was left to him between devout practice of his fervent faith and what might be discreetly described as romantic gallantry. This marked him down as a local wonder, for the ordinary Catholic in the pew of those days was depressingly convinced that these activities were incompatible. The effect on the ladies of Newcastle, especially those whose upbringing had not been disciplined by the stern logic of Catholic principles, was less condemnatory. Indeed it might more truthfully be said that it was tinged with enthusiasm and more truthfully still, with downright susceptibility. And lucky it was, for though his ardour was sincere while it lasted, it did not last very long.

No doubt—I admit I can only guess—no doubt he rewarded their attachment with the usual favours, red roses at breakfast, candlelit suppers, perhaps even an occasional stroll on the Town Moor. What was out of the ordinary was that he also treated them to an intensive course in the great truths of the faith. And very persuasive he must have been, for as he delicately began to slip the cable of one attachment he would bring her to the harbour of my uncle's study, before putting out to sea in search of another. It was only after several ladies had been successfully instructed and received into the Church that my uncle, who was a man of great simplicity, began to smell a rat.

The treasure of the faith was never a bargaining counter but always a parting gift. And to my uncle's wonderment these unlikely conversions stuck. Indeed they led to exemplary lives distinguished by regular attendace at Mass and the sacraments, prayer and charitable works. None, said my uncle, who was not so simple that he was blind to human fickleness, had ever fallen away.

And so, where another man of similar disposition might in Bernard Miles's words "have spread his maker's image about a bit", the Russian Count's trophies were souls devoted to God in this life and amply prepared for heaven. Which, I suspect, gave my uncle some funny feelings when he looked out on his congregation of a Sunday morning and left me with the conviction that God is less like *Bradshaw's Railway Timetable* than—well—like the current timetable for British Rail's Network South. And you cannot be more unreliable than that.

WIT AND WORSHIP

In my younger days church worship provided only accidental entertainment. Mostly a fairly simple humour was the order of the day: the canon absentmindedly sitting on his biretta; priests swaying onto the sanctuary for a High Mass with the broken rhythm of a line of camels; Sr Ribena darting out like a tiny motor torpedo boat to retrieve a fallen vase of flowers or rescue a foundering candle. But now and again, heights of rapture were achieved. There was the time the church organist pulled the wrong stop on his electric organ and filled the church with the sound of barking dogs and trilling nightingales; or the blacker humour of the day a curate began his sermon: "In a little while you shall see me, and in a little while you shall see me not", and promptly suited his actions to his words by dropping dead in the pulpit.

But by and large worship was a sombre business and we were left in no doubt that we attended in a spirit of stern duty, not for amusement. The ground note of most church worship, it seemed to me as a child, was sin and sadness. The hymns were suffused with Victorian melancholy. One with a particular, plangent melody, little heard nowadays, seemed to encapsulate them all. "Darkening shadows fall around us, stars their silent watches keep; hush the heart oppressed with sorrow, dry the tears of them that weep." War, and the absences caused by war, poverty, austerity, fed the ache at the heart of that singing. Church worship gave it a steady focus, a context for its expression.

These days the tone has undergone a marked change. The spirit of modern liturgy is more robust, more hopeful, more imaginative, more surprising. The resurrection is to the forefront, alleluias drown out the beating of breasts, cheerfulness keeps breaking in. Anyone who comes out of, for example, a folk Mass crowded with young people supposedly abandoning church-going in large numbers, is likely to leave with the feeling that the world is a good place to be in rather than with an urge to slink into a corner and die.

Yet the new liturgy has its own threads of accidental humour to satisfy the mordant. Especially those bidding prayers which seem to imply that the Almighty has mislaid his omniscience; situation reports from earth to heaven. "Lord, the housing list in East Pillington is 34 per cent longer than it was last year and the council is reducing its grant because of government cuts. We ask you to deal with the matter by next Tuesday. Lord hear us." And the rich cocktail of plainsong, grand opera, pop tunes, dance and mime needs careful mixing if it is to illuminate and elevate instead of causing glassy-eyed embarrassment. I especially relish the story of an extremely conservative American archbishop who found himself presiding at the Eucharist in a parish with a dashing liturgical committee. Just after the gospel, a thin artificial mist began to creep across the chancel and out of it danced a young lady miming the descent of the Holy Spirit on the apostles. The archbishop turned to the parish priest and muttered frostily: "When she asks for a head on a plate it's gonna be yours."

Personally I relish a liturgy in which a whole range of arts and talents is put to the service of explaining and embellishing the central act of Christian worship and the wonderful works of God; and accept that some of the visual and auditory aids will not appeal to all tastes. The problem, if there is a problem, lies not in the occasional injury to refined sensibilities, or the harnessing of popular arts to the service of the altar—which has a long tradition to justify it—but the assumption that if worship is *not* entertaining, *not* uplifting, above all to our own taste, it is not worth taking part.

That is wrong, it seems to me, for two reasons. The first because the Eucharist especially is a deed, not a branch of theatre. God's deed, the meaning of all meanings, complete and effective whether ritually framed in paste or diamonds, piercingly moving or dull as ditch-water. Our forefathers' indifference to the "how" as opposed to the "what" of worship, had its point.

The second, less obvious reason is that it is the only act, the only place, where we can adequately confirm the foundation on which we base our lives, our vision of existence, the values we live by, the hopes we nurse, and the nature of our destiny. It is *the* act, *the* place, where we publicly express what we believe it means to be human. And as the painter feels the urge to put his work on public display, the athlete to compete, the mother to see the cake she has baked eaten by her family, we too need publicly to demonstrate the point of our lives. God's deed on the one hand, our deed on the other. Both worth dressing up and placing under spotlights. But our privilege to share in even when the costumes are laid away and the spotlights are dimmed. Still something to be done, even when the thrills are missing and the laughter too.

THE THINGS OF THIS WORLD

To compare the sublime with the ridiculous, the demands of a Christian life are frequently reminiscent of an old shaving-soap advertisement which read: Not too little, not too much, but just right. Whether the issue concerns belief or behaviour, the Christian is continually asked to perform a high-wire act, striking a balance between two extremes. He can, for example, topple one way by holding that Christ is only divine, or the opposite way by holding that Christ is only human, instead of walking the fine line of orthodoxy that declares him to be both fully divine and fully human. And once that mistake is made, it will be no surprise if he follows it through by asserting that man should be pure in spirit or is mere matter, rather than both sharing the divine nature and being of the earth earthy; or that the Church is either a wholly divine institution unsullied by human imperfection or merely one human organisation among many, like Shell Oil, rather than a community uniquely graced by divine life yet made up of fallible, peccable human beings and consequently flawed, like every human organisation, by weakness and error.

Much the same kind of balancing-trick is needed in our attitude towards this world and the things of this world, the world where we live our brief mortal lives, the world which is also the stage for the great drama of redemption. It is one of the great ironies of life that Christians have the reputation of caring little for this world, preferring to stand at the edge of its pleasures and excitements and lambast the dangers of worldliness rather than plunge in and enjoy them. Yet the enthusiasm of the innocent worldly is often truer to the fundamental belief of Christians about the nature of this world, created by the Father redeemed by the Son and indwelt by the Holy Spirit, a world graced by the presence of God-made-man and whose pleasures as well as whose sufferings he has experienced and enjoyed. There is no theological justification for the unbending puritanism and unlovely drabness that is the hallmark of so many who call themselves Christian. On the contrary, as Vatican II's pastoral constitution on the Church in the modern world expresses it, "Redeemed by Christ and made a new creature by the Holy Spirit, man can, indeed he must, love the things of God's creation: it is from God that he has received them and it is as flowing from God's hand that he looks upon them and reveres them".

While Christians need to be sensitive to the sufferings and deprivation that warp so many human lives, and equally sensitive to the fact that all the good things of this world are only on temporary loan, these are no grounds for failing to relish and delight in the phenomena of the natural world or the marvellous achievements in art and science of man himself and the rich variety of human experience laid open to us during our time on earth. Loving the things of this world needs no apologies; not to love them is an insult to their creator.

What distinguishes, or should distinguish, the Christian from the unbelieving worldly, is not the degree of their relish for the good things of this world, though if anything the Christian has profounder reasons for keener delight. The difference lies rather in the different importance they attach to possessions and their contrasting reaction to the temporary or permanent denial of the things they enjoy.

Spiritual writers call this Christian characteristic "detachment" or "indifference", both of them, unfortunately, words that have a bleak, negative ring. Yet they are shorthand for the very positive attitude described in the same pastoral constitution when it goes on: "Man thanks his divine benefactor for all these things and enjoys them in a spirit of poverty and freedom: thus he is brought to a true possession of the world, as having nothing yet possessing everything: 'All things are yours; and you are Christ's; and Christ is God's'."

In practice, this means that the Christian can delight in created things without being slave to an obsessive compulsion to possess them; can relish a fine painting, fine furniture or a fine house, can enjoy a splendid garden or landscape, without feeling his pleasure is frustrated unless he owns them. And still more, knows that if his circumstances prevent the enjoyment of such things or if by chance he loses them, his essential human worth and dignity are in no way diminished, that there is no place for vexation and envy, that his life is still worthwhile and worth living. It is to accept with genuine tranquillity that the Lord gives and the Lord takes away, or sometimes does not give at all. It is to hang free towards the things of this world, delighting in them when they are available, but losing neither peace of mind nor self-esteem when they are not. It is true poverty of spirit, the ultimate freedom.

LIVING WITH LENT

During the second World War, a friend tells me, an inventive soldier felt that his part in the war effort was not getting the credit it deserved. So he designed and built a Morale Machine. When it was fastened to the shoulders and switched on, an artificial arm patted him on the back while a mechanical voice repeated "You're a jolly good chap. You're a jolly good chap." Such machines, I fancy, were they on the market, would sell like hot cakes during Lent. It has been preserved, along with Christmas, dehydrated, by those who have no relish for Christian belief. Each is a feast with a hole in the middle, its customs cherished, the cause of it all forgotten. "Given it up for Lent, old boy" rumbles the city gent, with a nod to the brandy and cigars. "Given it up for Lent" simper the office girls, waving away the Kit-Kats and eclairs. And in the pause that follows a ghostly arm descends and a ghostly voice declares "You're a jolly good chap. You're a jolly good girl."

Self-congratulation follows self-discipline as a hangover follows moonshine. The Lord's command to do good works in secret gently fades, as the kettle drum and trumpet thus bray out the triumph of their pledge. As Ida Gorres notes in that remarkable biography *The Hidden Face,* Therese of Lisieux made some tart remarks on the subject. Ascetic efforts directed not towards God but one's own perfection were nothing but spiritual beauty culture. "The penitence that depresses us comes from vanity: penitence from God lifts our courage."

That is one pitfall. Another is choosing penances that make life a misery to others. Every religious fears the colleague enchanted to asceticism; it is like sharing a car with a drunken driver. As an old saying has it: "All Jesuits are saints or martyrs. The martyrs are those who live with the saints." When I was a small boy I remember falling under the spell of Willie Doyle, the Irish Jesuit who collected penances as other enthusiasts collect lead soldiers. Advancing years taught me that while he was rolling in the nettles one of his brethren was probably grumpily taking his classes.

Laypeople, too, become radioactive when penance infects them—like the girl undergraduate at Oxford who gave up talking for Lent. In a matter of days she reduced the whole college to a blubbering, tearful fury, as she refused to acknowledge requests to Pass the Salt. And in how many Catholic homes must the scene in my grandfather's household have been annually repeated. Each Lent he gave up his pipe. At the end of the first week the wife of his bosom with their nine children clinging to her skirts flung themselves at his feet, beating the ground with their foreheads and imploring him to return to the self-indulgence which so admirably became him. Broken by these pleas he repossessed his pipe. After a few puffs his brow unclouded, his eyes cleared, benignity suffused him, the household was again filled with joy and laughter.

On the whole, as we wave goodbye to the statutory penances that Catholics wore like football favours, the Church's present concern to accentuate the positive can be welcomed. The new penance trails no clouds of glory. Giving up drink, novels or chocolate biscuits pales beside the effort to give up prejudice, fears and fantasies. Even if we stop short of the old Catholic lady who claimed that she never shook hands with Protestants or members of the middle classes, we can always ask ourselves who we won't shake hands with. There are faithless fears for ourselves, our nation, the Church, even for mankind itself, to be pruned by hope and courage; the fantasies woven about our own capacities, ambitions, and fulfilment, needing to be dusted down. Plenty of room for giving up there, and with more purpose.

Then, too, there are those whose penance is involuntary and endemic. The sick, the hungry, the homeless, the imprisoned, and above all those who live in the shadow of all-powerful governments, forced to speak in whispers, threatened by torture and worse, with no protection in law. Former President Carter's emphasis on human rights was a hopeful sign, an overdue recognition that their promotion is the central human cause, and their denial the seed of all kinds of mischief. But the man at the helm cannot achieve much if the crew lie sleeping on the deck. Lent is a good time to shake off self-obsession and show we care for the rights of others, for the human chances of others, not only in declarations and noble sentiments but deeds. Joining Amnesty International, writing to or on behalf of prisoners of conscience, may need more self-conquest than giving up sweets. It may lack the sweet satisfaction of choosing our own penance but give heart to those caught in life's threshing machines. The kettledrum and trumpets will not bray out on earth, but I suspect the angels will rejoice in heaven.

A MORAL FOR ALL SEASONS

Besides its central character and theme, the Passion narrative is packed with sub-plots and walk-on parts reflecting a number of enduring human dilemmas and characteristic ways of responding to them. Perhaps the most vivid of these is the story of the Trial of Jesus before Pilate. Especially in its longest version, that of St John, it can be read like a perfectly crafted short story or viewed in the mind's eye as a tragic one-act film mounting by swift, seemingly inexorable, steps to the kind of climax that inspires only a horrified silence.

The story is in fact the antithesis of one of the most haunting of classic films, *Twelve Angry Men*. In that, you may remember, one member of a jury closeted together to consider their verdict after a murder trial finds himself alone in doubting the guilt of the accused. The heat, both literally and figuratively, is on him. To the rest it is an open and shut case. All are fretting to get out of the stifling jury room and back to normal life; their homes, their businesses or a ball-game. Though a man's life is at stake, heat, inconvenience, irritability, press them to make their decision without delay or probing the evidence too deeply. Quietly and courteously, the odd man out resists the pressure to fall in with the consensus. Little by little he communicates his doubts and little by little swings them over to his side. Through one man's integrity and conviction, justice is done.

The story of Pilate travels in the opposite direction. The decision he has to make is not illuminated by the hindsight of Christian piety. With that hindsight he can be seen as a human being passing judgement on his creator, a worldly authority sentencing the Son of God to death. But it was not like that at the time. Nor was he faced with plucking the truth out of a welter of conflicting evidence. He is quick to conclude that the prisoner before him is innocent. He was not sifting right from wrong. His challenge is to do what he knows without doubt to be right.

It is a familiar dilemma. And by turns he employs all the familiar commonplace ways of shuffling off personal responsibility. He questions, even ridicules, the charge. He claims that he is being asked to act *ultra vires:* he directs the case to Herod. He passes the buck—back to the chief priests, to the crowd clamouring for Christ's death. It is their problem, not his: why bring it to him? He tries half-measures—perhaps a small injustice, having Christ flogged, will conciliate the crowd and prevent the greater injustice of a death sentence. He appeals to the crowd's better nature, seeks to move them to pity—Behold the man. He tries to shock them into caution—would you have me crucify your King? But however he bobs and weaves, the accusers remain implacable and the responsibility of decision is forced back on him.

As his resolution weakens, he appeals to Christ himself for help. But from that silent figure no special help is forthcoming. It is as if God were saying, "You already know enough, you already know what to do. I will neither force your hand nor make it easy for you."

94

And so he begins to crack. The usual pressures begin to mount: the fear of giving offence, the fear of resulting disturbance, the fear of seeming incompetent, and worse still, as the crowd presses on his weakest spot, the fear of seeming politically unreliable, of blighting his own career, perhaps even of hazarding his own life. Against these earthly calculations the uneasiness he feels in the presence of Christ, the strange warning from his wife, the likely weight on his conscience, the penalty that may attach to doing injustice, seem remote and insubstantial. His conviction is less valuable than his hide. All that is left to him is to diminish his offence in his own mind and to distance himself from it by the gesture of washing his hands. And so, as Luke describes in a single chilling sentence, "He released the man who had been thrown into prison for insurrection and murder, whom they asked for; but Jesus he delivered up to their will."

There is too much of Pilate in everyman to be hard on him. A man of the world might even say he did not do too badly to hold out so long. Yet the very familiarity of his behaviour, the sneaking sympathy it engages together with its appalling consequences, is precisely what makes his story so disturbing. In private, at work, in public office, the conflict between conviction and wanting to save one's skin runs through life like a dark thread. The pressures may not be so dramatic, perhaps only the desire not to seem troublesome, or too noticeable, or eccentric. In the everyday world it is easier to be Pilate than the honest juror. But for the Christian believer the figure of Pilate is a perpetually haunting presence, an uncomfortable reminder that as well as a clear head and a warm heart, the Christian needs a strong backbone.

MY FEARS FOR THE CHURCH

Catholics of my generation have long been familiar with the charge that Communism, Fascism and Catholicism are birds of a feather, three competing ideological systems with the same totalitarian characteristics: heavily centralised, making worldwide claims to power, and imposing a rigid doctrinal orthodoxy through an administrative apparatus demanding uncritical allegiance. Against this charge the short answer has been that the Church has no guns, no concentration camps, no firing squads; the longer answer that the Roman Curia is not a Politburo, the Church's officials not a *nomenklatura,* the Catholic faith not an ideology, that Catholic orthodoxy does not demand intellectual sterility, nor religious obedience abandonment of personal integrity.

Even so the charge creates feelings of unease. A thousand personal experiences may convince that it is false, yet one is bound to ask why outsiders should even be tempted to make such a comparison. Why do they see on the balconies of the Kremlin, the Heavenly Palace and St Peter's Square three sets of interchangeable men sharing the same authoritarian mentality? Why do they pick up the same bad vibrations from the way the three systems run their affairs?

The nastiest feature of the present crisis in the Church, certainly the worst in my lifetime, is that it is steadily reinforcing this distasteful comparison. And, ironically, it is at the very moment when totalitarian political systems are being totally discredited that the new Ultramontanists seem hell-bent on displaying the same shameful mentality and methods of management. Why is the Soviet system falling apart? Because no central authority can run an empire without wholesale delegation of decision-making sensitive to local needs and circumstances. Because a *nomenklatura* of party hacks chosen for their pliability rather than their competence cannot function either humanely or efficiently and is scorned by decent people with some degree of self-respect. Because no system can long evade realities, however unwelcome, and eventually must come to terms with them. Because no system can keep stoning its men of vision, silencing its thinkers, snuffing out every enterprise which is not an official initiative of the party, without becoming sterile and arthritic. And because no system can sustain its prevailing orthodoxy by constantly rewriting history and whatever doctrinal history does not suit its book. By doing these things it loses all trust and respect, all listeners and followers.

These things are clear enough when they affect others. But they are equally true closer to home. They are as true of Churches as of political parties. Rome's answer to totalitarian political systems cannot be to create a religious equivalent as a counter-weight. It cannot centralise power at the expense of neutering local Churches in closer touch with local realities. It cannot without disaster create a *nomenklatura* of bishops and other senior officials who are neither trusted nor respected by the people they are meant to inspire, and whose chief characteristic is that they are temperamental doormats. No one of ability and integrity will serve in such a role.

It cannot publicly humiliate or disparage saints, prophets and pastors commanding the love and admiration of millions — its Camaras, Arns and Romeros — silence its most thoughtful and respected theologians, suffocate every spark of new life which springs up unbidden, without calling into question its whole value

96

system and inviting the belief that naked power rather than spiritual insight and pastoral concern is its chief preoccupation. It cannot impose a non-historical orthodoxy and dismiss the most complex, intractable questions of the day with pious cliches, without inviting derision. It cannot acknowledge the Holy Spirit only within a small coterie, dimissively contradict the living experience of its own faithful, reduce the life of the spirit to a matter of religious observances, without surrendering the right to be heard. It cannot preach a Gospel of resurrection by clinging to a dead past. It cannot shut out disturbing realities, disturbing ideas, disturbing people, without itself becoming a mausoleum.

Things may not yet have reached quite such a pass. But the threat is unmistakable. The totalitarian charge looks more plausible, the defence is harder to mount convincingly. The time for quiet diplomacy is past, and so too, at every level of the Church, for "obedience", "meekness" and "discretion" as a cover for what is in fact sheer spinelessness. Such public abuse of authority demands a public solidarity movement of resistance from the local Churches, which are not branch offices of a corporation headquarters, but each the Church in its own place. A Church of craven bishops, cowed priests and listless people is a self-contradiction. It cannot afford to be thought of, even faintly, as a sort of ecclesiastical totalitarian state — rigid, fearful, shut-in, and dead, dead, dead.

A MEANNESS OF SPIRIT

As my friends know, I love England little short of idolatry, and return to these shores from wandering abroad like a rabbit to its burrow. Nowhere seems better than here. But even England is not the kingdom of light, happiness and peace which is the end of all our journeying. So all the more reason for admitting our faults (are we not proud of our truthfulness?), especially our prejudices (and our tolerance?) which lead to injustice (and our sense of fair play?). And more reason still in this age of despots, torturers and ideologues. If England does not champion human dignity, the poor creature may as well give herself up to the dragons.

If black people in Britain feel demeaned, scorned and shut out, where does our failure lie? First, perhaps, in a lack of imagination, and a lack of perspective, especially a convenient forgetfulness of history. Years ago I remember lying in hospital after a spinal operation. In the next bed to mine was a sixteen-year-old boy paralysed by polio from the neck down. In the next ward a man who had lost both legs and an arm in successive amputations. I kept telling myself that my own pain was nothing compared with theirs, and that I would soon be up and about again while their future was as bleak as could be. But my pain was *my* pain and these cheerful comparisons provided little comfort. The perspective, however, was objectively true, and it had some importance.

Similarly, for those who find life an uphill struggle, and especially for those who are badly housed, out of work or underpaid, it is easy to grow resentful of waves of immigrants and see them as rivals or even as the causes of one's own plight. Easy to say that charity begins at home, that we must look after our own, that we have our own problems without taking on outsiders'. Our pain is our pain, and blocks out the pain of others. But the perspective is still objectively wrong, or so I believe.

The first and foremost fact is that Britain is an ex-imperial power. The new immigrants are not intruders or wandering beggars; more like illegitimate offspring. A father of children born out of wedlock may argue that he was drunk at the time and had no intention of begetting them; or that they were lucky to be born of love and that he retains the kindliest affection for them. What he cannot do is deny all further responsibility and shut his door to them. Britain is roughly in the same position. The Empire may or may not have been a good thing. It is too early to write its history and draw up a final balance sheet. It was built by good and bad men alike; and for mixed motives. Hard men helped to fashion it who would casually shoot the natives when they started to get uppish; and also district commissioners who worked themselves into the grave in a spirit of total selflessness. What can scarcely be disputed is that wealth flowed from the colonial tributaries into Britain and not vice versa; and that the offspring remain, very poor compared with their affluent parent. There is a debt to be paid, and a responsibility to be shouldered. We cannot wash our hands of the past. And we can pay for the wealth, the commodities and raw materials, the treasures from distant lands, that have poured into Britain during its imperial centuries, either by giving the ex-colonial peoples enough to help them stand on their own feet (which we are far from doing), or making our homes their own.

Part of the perspective is also the fact that by any yardstick one chooses to employ—average income, life expectancy, health, employment rates, social services and benefits—Britain is still a privileged nation. The present economic thunderclaps should not drown out the cries of pain from worse off areas of the world. When a trade union proposes strike action to insist on the right to work it is victim of a false assumption which bedevils the whole country. A need to work, yes. But a right to work? Who can guarantee that? And relative to what and to whom? Has the British workman a divine right to work greater than the African or the Indian? Or, enlarging the canvas, have the British a divine right to retain and improve their standard of living no matter how badly off their fellow-men abroad? The blunt answer is no — and we can still pare off a good deal of fat to help those poorer than ourselves without coming near the poverty of those in countries where over a third of the population are permanently jobless.

Just as the new black immigrants show up, like an X-ray in reverse, the areas of deprivation and unfairness in our society, so too they call attention to the narrowness of vision and the meanness of spirit which distort our view of today's world. What the resentful bigots require is not appeasement but education. They have lost their sense of proportion. Whatever the pains of those who think like them, they can scarcely be sharper than the pains of those driven by poverty to seek refuge in Britain, and finding themselves resented, cold-shouldered, done down, and yet expected to adopt values and standards higher than those of the indigenous Whites. It is not time to pride ourselves on our charity—we can only be shamed by our injustice.

SAINTS IN ASPIC

It was my great good fortune to be, like so many of my generation, brought up on *Six O'Clock Saints*—along of course with children's comics like the *Beano* and the *Wizard* and other tales of mystery and imagination free of any overt sanctifying purpose. That little book and its sequel, by Joan Wyndham, led me forever to connect saints with excitement. There was St. Aloysius creeping across the barrack square in the hour of the siesta and firing off a cannon and bringing his father's artillerymen tumbling out of their beds thinking there were enemies at the gate. And St Nicholas, an early Sherlock Holmes, who guessed that a barrel of pickled pork was three chopped-up little boys and with a mighty blessing brought them hopping out of the brine and back to life to the great embarrassment of a wicked innkeeper. And the juggler-saint who juggled and danced before a statue of Our Lady because he had nothing else to offer. And St. Tarcisius, stealing through the streets with the blessed sacrament like an undercover agent for the Roman resistance. They all made their mark in the innocent years before one had heard of the Bollandists, and made the painful discovery that the only acceptable truths are those you can hit with a hammer; the painful discovery, too, that grown-ups preferred their saints to be like Antonia White's nun, "very beautiful in a way that was both spiritual and witty and dying of consumption."

I sometimes think that the medieval hagiographers, piling their Pelions of miracles on their Ossas of legend, did sanctity a greater service than their Counter-Reformation counterparts—whether scholars who strip saints down to the bone, or the sanctimonious whose saints are merely bundles of interchangeable virtues devoid of personality. In some curious way good and honourable intentions have steered us towards the present time when saints are thought to be boring, and to call someone a saint is the deadliest of insults. The quickest way to ruin a man's career is to call him a bit of a saint. And the very word "saint" in front of an honest name seems a kind of diminishment. Canonisation acts like a vacuum system once common to old-fashioned stores; put a name in the brass canister, pull the handle, and whoosh, another admirable human being serviceable to the human community has been translated to realms where we cannot think to follow. I felt this even of the English martyrs: Edmund Campion, Edward Arrowsmith, and Margaret Clitherow were our countrymen, close at hand, haunting the same thoroughfares, faced with familiar dilemmas, and not too rarified to be good company; but St Edmund Campion, St Edward Arrowsmith and St Margaret Clitherow were all of a sudden mere wisps of vapour.

Something, it seems, is wrong, when nothing comes off the canonisation assembly line but monks and mother foundresses all as indistinguishable as chunks of processed cheese. Perhaps the whole process has become too precious, too finicky, too centralised and too austere when only one kind of Christian can reach the altars of the Church, and that here is another area where some degree of decentralisation would be worthwhile. In Fosco Maraini's book *Secret Tibet* he remarks: "It is a fact that one's relations with people are to a large extent at the level of the subconscious. Vague hints and intuitions reinforce the feeling we have about people that they are either good or bad. Lama Tendar emanates peace and benevolence almost as if they were physical realities; he radiates an inner light." That is not too bad a basis for *vox populi* acclamation of the holy ones among us. The strict logic of the canonisation process no more expresses the peculiar quality that marks the very good from the truly holy, than the canon law of matrimony expresses the inner reality of marriage. Very few of us, I imagine, cannot think of people among our lifetime's acquaintance who bear this peculiar stamp of the holy, and have not been touched and inspired by it, a stamp which often coexists with comfortably human failings and limitations. Yet somehow these everyday saints are excluded by the system from being put into universal circulation to hearten all the people of God; and those bevies of mother foundresses practising rarified virtues in a rarified atmosphere distort the definition of sanctity and appear to make it unattainable in the ordinary life of home, office, school and factory. It will be a good day when the mother who has raised a family without slaying her offspring, or Fred the milkman who has never missed his daily round, have as good a chance of acclamation as those whose virtues are more cloistered; when there are bank-clerk saints, and factoryhand saints, and footballer saints, and even, God save the mark, city-gent or shop steward saints, as well as monk saints and nun saints. Our own age is, I believe, as rich in its variety of saints as another, and it is a pity that canonisation has become such a needle's eye through which only one shape of saint can pass.

Doubly a pity when the saint whom Pius X called "the greatest saint of modern times," Thérèse of Lisieux, has brought to light the ordinariness of sanctity (which is far from saying its drabness) and drawn it within the scope of every man. It is an irony that she, as twentieth-century in her doubts, confusions and dark despairs as any contemporary agnostic, has been sanitised and homogenised to conform with the official regulations, just as the strong six-foot woman, artful and comical, has been most untruthfully shrunk to a petite, simpering, pietistic consumptive. Happily, the intuition of the faithful has once again reached through the lucubrations of the hagiographers to the truth at the core, and grasped her message in a most astonishing way. But official theory and practice still has a long way to go to catch up if the popular notion of sanctity in the world at large is to undergo a long overdue refurbishment. The essence of the matter is that saints can be anywhere, and every human activity can be the stuff of sanctity. Conditions and professions do not count. Neither does temperament; saints can be quirky, frugal, extravagant, shy, flamboyant. What they cannot be is boring—and if the system makes them so, it is the system that should go.

FAITH'S CENTRAL MYSTERY

The Most High, Most Holy and Most Blessed Trinity, to use the kind of divine title beloved of Christian mystics, is incontrovertibly the ultimate and profoundest mystery of faith. All Christian doctrine flows out of and returns to that mystery. Nothing is so clearly a revelation, nothing so evidently not cooked up by the human reason and imagination. Yet it cannot be claimed that this crucial understanding of God figures prominently in the average sermon list or slips easily into the conversation when Christians gather to ruminate on their beliefs. Theological treatments of the subject often read like analyses of family ties in a Celtic rural community (perhaps the most baffling of all human puzzles), while the occasional pulpit skirmish with the subject rarely gets beyond a lame declaration that it is all a mighty mystery which no doubt we shall understand in heaven but which need not fever our brains overmuch on earth. It has nothing to do, they seem to insinuate, with digging holes in the road, tapping away at a computer, or doing the washing-up.

The mystics certainly must be excluded from this rough judgement. For them all prayer and reflection leads into deeper exploration and understanding of the life of the Trinity, to seeing it reflected in the created world, and to sharing that life in the ordinary occupations of the daily round. Twice I have been allowed to glimpse that this is not just the high-falutin' talk of esoterics who live in a higher gear than most of us. Both were on improbable occasions, the first during an *al fresco* luncheon in a farmhouse garden when bang in the middle of the festivities the elderly French mother of the assembled family suddenly launched into a disquisition on the Trinity, its meaning and place in Christian life, that could only have issued from a lifetime's meditation on the subject and would have left even an English bishop gasping for breath. The second was during a tour of the university campus in Manchester, when somewhere along the Oxford road my priest companion suddenly exposed the way in which his understanding of the Trinity had shaped and directed his own pastoral work and spiritual life. Though the details of these discourses now escape me, both left the strongest possible impression that the Trinity is not inescapably beyond the human horizon, but touches our human life at every point.

So we should expect. If we are made in the image of God, we are made in the image of the Trinity; and the life of the Trinity must in some sort be reflected in the pattern of our human life. Perhaps one such reflection is between the activities identified with each person of the Trinity and the no doubt only blurredly separable but nevertheless distinguishable categories of activity in which we engage. Thus to the Father is credited all that we understand by generation, creation, maintenance; and much of our human activity can be seen as cooperation in that work. Everything we do to awaken and cherish new life, to fashion, mould and develop our physical environment, shares in that work of the Father; fathering and mothering, designing and building, growing crops and breeding cattle, shaping and tending the landscape, manufacturing, organising, fashioning all kinds of things for our use and delight, all crafts, arts and technologies, in short every kind of making, fall under this head.

Likewise, all human works of compassion, healing, reconciliation, sacrifice, forgiveness, making amends, and making good again reflect the work of redemption and reconciliation identified most closely with the Son. All that is, to use the current jargon, that falls under the head of caring.

And finally, the special role of the Holy Spirit is reflected in every positive idea and inspiration, however slight and humble, in every advance in knowledge and wisdom, in every flash of imagination, in every movement of the heart. The artist, lover, philosopher and inventor may embody and express this area of human experience most richly, but there is no one to whom it is foreign, for it covers the simplest ideas and feelings as well as the most elaborate.

To divide these categories of activity into neat compartments would clearly make no better sense than attempting to saw the Trinity into three pieces. In common experience they are functions of the same human identity and intertwine, influence and complement each other. There, too, perhaps there is a glimpse of the essential unity of the three persons of the Trinity. But in these times, when so many people feel fragmented and divided within themselves, and find it difficult to recognise or work to any clear pattern of life, at least there are here suggestive hints of the contact between the Trinity's life and our own. Hints and glimpses worth brooding on, a shape and sense of direction to all our human activities, as we journey into the future.

SIGNS AND WONDERS

O world invisible, we view thee,
O world intangible, we touch thee,
O world unknowable, we know thee,
Inapprehensible, we clutch thee.

Francis Thompson's lines are a succinct expression of what is special about the Christian faith. Man, faced with the enigma of his own nature and destiny, the mystery of the world in which he finds himself living, racked by the contradictions and inconsistencies of his everyday experience, puzzled about the nature of his relationship with whatever power lies behind the visible world, suddenly finds a hand being extended to him from the other side. The answer to the question 'What is God like?' is given him in terms which he can understand; a mirror is placed in his hands in which he can see and understand himself.

'He who has seen me has seen the Father'. That is the basic premise of our faith. If it is not true then no light has broken upon the people who sit in darkness. If it is not true we cannot claim to have cracked the riddle of existence; we can only shrug our shoulders in face of a life which has no apparent point or meaning. It is only the light of Christ, with a face and body like ours, speaking human words and performing familiar actions, which can turn our night into day. Through him alone we can take hold of the invisible and intangible, make sense of what is by nature infinite and unfathomable. Through him alone we can arrive at the conclusion that there is firm ground to stand on, absolute truths which mark out a path through the wilderness. 'If it were not so I would have told you'; only one voice has ever spoken with that degree of certainty, only one man ever offered convincing proof that he has the right to speak in such a fashion.

The Word was made flesh and dwelt amongst us. God, dwelling amongst us. God, dwelling in inaccessible light, steps into the arena of the visible world, and lives visibly among his own creatures. His power and presence, his operations within the world, his 'personality', are no longer just a matter for speculation and guesswork; the door is open, the lights are burning, the fire is glowing in the hearth.

The Word was made flesh, the Word was made visible. And just as God made himself visible in Christ, tangible, clutchable, so his power and presence are made visible and tangible in our own times. In the Church which is the visible community that Christ brought into being two thousand years ago, in its central activity, the Mass, in the bread of life which he gives us to eat, in the living word of the Scriptures, in the signs that we call sacraments, and in each other—temples of the Holy Spirit. Through these we may not know all there is to be known about God; but we know enough.

'Let me hold it!' Every parent knows that children are rarely satisfied until they have got their hands on anything that catches their curiosity. It may be a baby, a butterfly, or a watch. Whatever it is, they want to touch it, get the feel of it, possess it at least for a moment or two. And the instinct does not pass away with childhood. One only has to go round a museum or a stately home to be confronted with notices at every turn saying, 'Please do not touch'. The classical tag of scholastic philosophy that nothing is known except through the senses sums up one of the most easily observed of all human characteristics.

The Gospels contain many incidents showing this instinct at work; the woman with the issue of blood touching the hem of Jesus's garment; Magdalen clasping his feet when she meets him in the garden after his rising from the dead; Thomas insisting on touching the wounds in Christ's hands and side to make sure that he is not a ghost. And our Lord must often have felt hands reaching out for him, just as people today try to shake hands with a modern politician while he is passing among them.

In a sense, the sacraments are God's way of meeting this need. It is true that he could act on us and be among us quite invisibly. Often God does influence us in ways that we cannot see, for the spirit blows where it will and is not bound to act in ways that are predictable and, so to speak, official. But God respects our human need to know through the senses, to lay hold of him, to reach out and touch him, even in some fashion to possess him. And so he comes to meet us in visible forms to give us positive assurance that virtue is coming out of him and entering us. He does so through humble and familiar things; water, wine, oil, bread, the actions and gestures of men appointed to act in his name, things that we can eat and drink and see and touch. All the sacraments are an answer to the plea of God's children: Let me hold it, let me touch. They continue the process of making his power and presence visible, which began when he came among us as a visible man. There is nothing superstitious in the Church's understanding of these signs. They do not deny the possibility that God can and may act upon us directly in ways not visible to the senses and without working through human instruments. But for human beings it would be a bleak and disturbing world if his power and presence were a matter of continual guesswork, and if we could never point with any certainty at something which lies within reach of our senses and say 'the finger of God is here'. The sacraments are not primitive rituals, magical practices through which we try to make God our servant, but the footprints that mark his passage through our daily life.

It is not uncommon to hear people expressing disappointment with the sacraments. They do not feel they receive, or at least do not experience, the benefits they have been led to expect. There is no sudden inrush of faith, no sense of greater well-being, no fresh capacity to pray or to see clearly the answers to troubling problems. But receiving a sacrament is not like stepping on a train which will then carry one unresisting to a set destination. It is more like turning on the ignition of a car, which puts power into our hands without deciding exactly what we are going to do with it. Like the miracles Christ performed during his public life, the sacraments respect human freedom. In each, God's presence and power were and are sufficiently revealed for men to recognise them. But by raising men from the dead, healing the sick, casting out demons, Christ did not overwhelm men to the point that they had willy-nilly to accept him. The sacraments likewise are not magical actions in either direction: God does not cast a spell over us, nor through them are we able to cast a spell over him. He offers us something, himself, which will enable us to use our full human autonomy in the wisest and most enlightened way. And we do not try to command God, like a genie released from a bottle, but express our faith in his power and presence, and our willingness to become the kind of creature that he has designed us to be. There is a free interchange, an offering and a response.

The sacraments are not only to do with renewal of faith in God and his saving events. They also involve renewal of faith in the value of the created world and the events that constitute a human life. By using the simple things of the earth: water, bread, wine, oil as the vehicles of his action, God helps us to see all these things in a new light. As precious, lovable, worthy of our care and respect. Like Gerard Manley Hopkins we can now see the world as 'charged with the grandeur of God' flaming out 'like the shining from shook foil'. And similarly the mysterious processes of human life, birth, marriage, human relationships, death are also viewed in a new light. Their essential soundness is affirmed, their goodness and importance is dramatised by God's own acknowlegement of them and his personal sharing in them. In a world where it is easy to see all life as pointless, all human activity as empty and fundamentally meaningless, the sacraments serve as continual reminders of the value and importance of everything that we are and do. They renew faith in ourselves. They tell us that we too are charged with the grandeur of God, and that in the simplest and most basic of all our human actions his grandeur can flame out. Nothing we do is merely secular, nothing unhallowed, but everything filled with his glory.

All about us lie objects whose ugliness lies not in themselves but in their setting. Diseases, weeds, rusty bicycles, all of them can reveal, however improbably, some strange particular beauty through the eye of the artist or the glass of the microscope. The world is crammed with things original and spare, if we cultivate the curiosity and take the time to look for them.

Children know that the world is full of wonders. Coming fresh to the world and enjoying a privileged freedom, unfretted by adult responsibilities and anxiety over the passage of time, they can linger over the oddity and interest of everything that lies in their path; from insects and pebbles to tarnished coins and abandoned cars. Their minds run easily to magic and fantasy because the real world of sun, moon and stars seems in their eyes to be already magical.

For the adult things can be very different. The sheer daily grind, the struggle for existence, can easily dull that child's sense of wonder. Everything seems familiar, dull, pedestrian, and scarcely worth more than passing notice. Even astonishing phenomena like television, space journeys, and the harnessing of nuclear energy, are quickly taken for granted. It is only too easy for this neutrality in face of the world's wonder to turn to contempt—and then nature reveals its own dramatic ways of answering back.

Neither the whole-hearted secularist who regards the world as a wasteland without meaning or purpose, nor the religious man who sees his religion as one element to be woven into the fabric of human existence, really offers much help. In their several ways each undervalues and misreads our total physical environment. Against these views the sacraments stand out as signs which continually recall us to the full richness of human beings and the created order in which they pursue their destiny. In each there is an interpretation of the supernatural and the natural, the infinite and the finite, the divine and the human. The meaning of each sacrament is not confined within itself, but points outward to the full truth about man and the world that he inhabits; namely that God penetrates the whole created order and is at work in every creature. Man, living creatures, every growing thing, the earth itself, all are touched with divinity. The heavens tell forth the work of his fingers, the earth bears the imprint of the Lord.

In our day when abuse of the earth and its resources causes anxiety about the future of man, and indeed his very capacity to go on existing, the need of reverence for creation is recognised by increasing numbers of people. Reverence springs out of wonder. It is something which Christians, familiar with the sacraments, should never have lost sight of. For these signs are the womb of wonder.

IN DEFENCE OF LIBERALISM

"For every boy and every girl that is born into the world alive is either a little Liberal or a little Conservative." Alter the capitals of Gilbert's original lines to lower case, and they seem as broadly true a categorisation of human outlooks as when they were written. There is a recognisably conservative and a recognisably liberal outlook, the one concerned with order, security and tradition, the other with freedom, risk and invention, and rooted, it would often seem, as much in temperament or experience of living as in academic theory. The conservative inclines, for what he believes to be good reasons, to subordinate persons to institutions; if he goes too far he creates a tyranny. The liberal subordinates institutions to persons; if he goes too far he sows the seeds of anarchy.

What seems to me to be a consistent phenomenon is that most politicians attract support by preaching liberal ideals and values but once in power to a greater or lesser extent adopt the conservative outlook. Few politicians would stand on a platform and boast of their illiberalism. Few would promise prospective voters less freedom, less dignity, less responsibility and fewer chances of prosperity. On the other hand ours is not and never has been, a liberal world. To accuse liberals, as conservatives frequently do, of being corrupters of the young and subverters of society is to part company with reality. The truth is that liberalism, as Chesterton said of Christianity, has not failed, it has never been tried. Looking at the realities of today's world, it is not liberals who run the armies, the security forces, the armaments factories, the torture schools and the death squads. Not liberals who level the forests, exhaust the fishing grounds, pollute the high seas. Not liberals who run the great financial institutions, the mega-corporations, the great bureaucracies, or with rare exceptions, the popular newspapers. It is not liberals who organise crime, run the drug rackets, the gambling and porno and prostitution. It is not liberals who send out armies to commit massacre and genocide. Behind all that lies an old old conservative principle—devil take the hindmost—and an old old conservative aim—to exalt the mighty and put down the humble.

Liberals have had few turns on the bridge and those mainly in Europe and not for long. Their familiar haunts are universities and like educational establishments, in the world of art, in a few newspapers and small magazines, and on the margins of politics. They may at times voice the aspirations and catch the ear of a very large audience, touch truths nursed in the hearts, awaken dreams, inspire visions. But they do not run the world. Few social processes start with the human person and try to design institutions to fit his nature and needs; all too many design institutions and, like Procrustes, force people to fit. The world is not run by people with compassion and respect for the many, concern for the weakest and most disabled human beings, a determination that as few human talents as possible should go to waste, a resolve that every human being should have a decent chance to better himself. It is run, for the most part, by people bent on acquiring wealth and power, or who have wealth and power and are determined to keep it. They will clap politely the peacemaker's speech before getting down to ordering mightier weapons. Clap the speech on social justice before planning to get some wretched peasants off a piece of wanted land.

Rich in kindness, consideration, cooperativeness though human beings are, these are not the qualities which first spring to mind when one considers the leaders and shapers of human society. The people at the top are at the top because they are not that kind of person. But when the citizenry protest, as protest they will, at the absence of kindness and consideration in some area of their lives, or when the earth protests at the battering it receives from predatory man, those who run the world find the liberal a useful scapegoat. It is a curious twist of logic and in a rough world the unkindest cut of all.

A WORD IN SEASON

My old school motto has teased and tantalised and itched away in my mind for over 40 years, ever since four impenetrable words on a theme book sprang to life in English. *Cor Numinis, Fons Luminis:* "Heart of Divinity, Fountain of Light". Wimbledon College's full name, never to my knowledge publicly employed, was and is the College of the Sacred Heart and it was this which inspired that extraordinary motto. And what a gift for life it is, arrowing straight into the intimate nature of God, the ultimate word about the ultimate reality.

Perhaps nothing in this world is more elusive than a notion of God that not only impresses the intellect but moves the affections. And here two archetypal symbols do just that. A heart and a fountain. Love and light. For many fastidious people the popular iconography of the Sacred Heart is distastefully crude. But what is it really saying? That the ultimate explanation for our vast creation, of this mystery of being of which we are part, is best symbolised by the human heart with all its homely and moving associations. That this incredible universe, growing almost yearly more awesome as scientists lay its remotest reaches and its most minute components open to the human eye, is the work of love: that indeed God is *L'amor che move il sole e l'altre stelle.* That we ourselves are the children of love. That the human love which we give and receive and prize above all other contentments flows out of and reflects the innermost core of the god-head. That in the experience of love, in all its expressions, we know most intimately, however imperfectly, what it is like to be God.

And Fountain of Light. Light without which our world is formless and we ourselves brought to a halt. And not only a candle in the dark, moonlight or starlight, or the rising sun bringing colour and shape to a world blanketed in darkness. But the light that through photosynthesis is vital to the growth of the myriad plants that delight the eye and feed the body. God is light and in him there is no darkness. And from that light flows the light that is essential for the very existence of life, and the light of understanding in which the point of life, its meaning, its purpose and direction, can, within our limited capacity, be grasped. Divine light, not artificial, not intermittent, seasonal, or subject to power cuts. But issuing from God as from a fountain ceaselessly playing, springing up endlessly and joyously, irradiating the uttermost parts of the universe, suffusing the darkest corners of the human heart. Intelligible God, intelligible Love, because "he who has seen me has seen the Father". Light because He who is Love came to be a light to all who sit in darkness and the shadow of death. God. *Cor Numinis, Fons Luminis.*

HOLINESS AND HUMANITY

I think it was Maurice Edelman who in one of his novels put into Disraeli's head the thought that the Church is the metaphor of an ordered society. No doubt in Disraeli's day notions of an ordered society were rather different from our own, though he himself can take some of the credit for the belief that social order must rest on fraternity and justice rather than hierarchy, rank, and coercion. But the observation is essentially a sound one, for the Church should indeed be a sign, a paradigm, a working model of what human society, viewed as a whole, might be. That is not to say it must be a society of full-blown saints, but that its motives and methods of action must be evidently those which make for sanctity. Not the hatred, greed, arrogance and worldly ambition which prompt so many human dealings, not the fears and narrowness, the jealousies and self-defensiveness that stifle so much human enterprise, but a loving respect for the human person, a joyful hope in human destiny, based on a brave faith in the God who made man and his world, and a secure trust that that world is a good place to be.

If the Church is the metaphor of an ordered society, perhaps it is true to say that the Pope is ideally the metaphor of the Church. Not some semi-divine Dalai Lama inviting superstitious awe: not a cosmic answering-machine with solutions to every conundrum; not a unique oracle through which the secrets of the godhead are continually transmitted; not, least of all, a supreme earthly authority to which every knee must bend: but a living epitome of Christian faith, joy, hope and sanity. This without doubt is the hardest thing to ask and the heaviest of all responsibilities — simply to embody what it means to be a Christian; and hardest of all to embody it naturally in the full glare of publicity. Harder, certainly, than filling the role of astute politician, efficient bureaucrat, brilliant apologist or electrifying orator. Yet it is what is most needed, and, I believe, what was felt to be most needed by a kind of universal instinct both inside and outside the Church. In a world of humbug and deviousness, of political conjuring tricks and underhand dealing, of commercial gimmicks and humbug, of heartless ideologies and headless sentiment, of lies and counter-lies that fly so thick they darken the sun, no authority can commend itself and no argument prevail except the living witness whose testimony is himself.

This surely is what the second Vatican Council was about — that the Church was inspired to realise how poor a witness it had come to be. Over several centuries of withdrawal from one great area of human enterprise and intercourse after another it had seemed to commend a way of life, a state of heart and soul, prim, anaemic, anxiety-ridden, epicene. And, truth to tell, its Popes reflected this, if not in their own persons, at least as their personalities, typed by ceremony and protocol, were allowed to register. The attitude of mind behind it totally divorced humanity from holiness, and in seeking to make the papacy sinless merely rendered it sterile.

The present Pope seems born to cure this ailing version of Christian life. The fact that he plays the guitar, sings songs and writes poetry, canoes and skis and climbs mountains, is not a curious accidental. It is an overdue recognition, at last embodied in a Pope, that Christian life demands an adventurous attempt to exercise the whole range of human powers, to live and relish a full human life. The fact that the man who embodies it has seen the cruel and corrupt side of human nature more painfully than most of us, lends it added point. He is the perfect visual aid to the central message of the council — that a sense of the transcendent and faith in the life to come should not cheapen the richness of human life on earth but add relish and flavour. And that the fruit of Christian faith and love and discipline is not a grouchy neurosis but a positive delight in the marvelous world about us and the company of fellow-men still more marvelously endowed. Holiness and true humanity are not alternatives, but the same.

WAITING

All of us, I suppose, find that much of our life is spent just waiting. We wait at bus stops, and on railway stations, often feeling listless and irritated by what seems a futile waste of precious time.

We wait impatiently for an important telephone call, letter or cheque, or, when we are ill, for the day the doctors tell us we can get up; and sometimes this kind of anxious waiting can prevent us from concentrating on anything else. We wait when we are bored for the five o'clock whistle, or just for 'something to turn up' which will relieve our monotony.

Then there are other and better kinds of waiting. There is the waiting which contains a special kind of joy, the joy of anticipation. It is experienced by the wife who looks forward to her husband's return from a journey, the family which waits for friends who are coming to dinner, the child waiting for the arrival of a promised present.

There is an even richer kind of waiting, a waiting which has a special point to it—waiting for the fulfilment of a process which has already begun. When we plant seeds in the garden we do not grudge the time spent waiting for flowers to appear: we know that time is needed for the seeds to ripen and the plants to grow.

The philosopher, the writer and the artist do not resent the time spent in apparently aimless brooding, when they know that a new idea is developing and taking shape. And, above all, the mother expecting a child knows that her time of waiting is not time wasted; she knows that the child within her is growing and coming close to the moment of birth.

The people of Israel knew all these emotions during the long years they were asked to wait for the coming of the Saviour. They were sometimes bored, anxious, impatient, at other times full of the joy of anticipation. Only gradually did the form in which God would reveal himself take shape.

Only gradually did their expectation of a Messiah, a national hero, give way to the expectation of a universal liberator for all creation, Emmanuel: In those days ten men out of nations speaking every language will seize hold of the robe of a single Jew and say: We will go with you, for we have heard that God is with you (Zacc. 8,23).

Theirs was a creative waiting. The stage was being prepared for God's entrance. His people were being given time to grow and mature, fitted to receive the Saviour among men. Their faith put down roots, their hope became the impulse of their lives.

And at last they saw God's promise fulfilled. We who live after Christ's coming are also asked to wait—for the completion of the kingdom, perhaps for some individual illumination or grace. With similar faith and hope we too can find that our waiting is creative.

'My soul awaits the Lord more eagerly than watchman waits for dawn'. The sentinel on the city wall watching the sky-line for the first light is a figure of Israel waiting for the coming of the Saviour.

He is an appealing figure. It is easy enough for us to share the feelings of a sentry at the end of the night, stiff, bored, blowing on his hands, longing for the moment when he can stand down.

There are many occasions when we have shared those feelings: at the end of a sleepless night, when we have been sick or in pain, bored or frustrated, or just gloomily waiting for inspiration. Even when we believe that relief is just round the corner we are never quite sure it will come.

It is not so easy to recapture Israel's expectation of a Saviour. We cannot artificially pretend that Christ has not come. But remembering Israel's time of waiting and the use the people made of it does have a point.

Even while they were wandering insecurely in the desert, or suffering captivity in Babylon, they were not only developing a sense of their personal relationship with God, but developing a clearer picture of the way in which their liberation would come.

All the time at least some of them stayed on the watch for their Saviour. And so when John the Baptist arrived on the scene there were people looking out for him. "Who are you?" they asked him. "Are you the Christ?" And he told them, "No".

In the same way, when Christ did come among them so shortly afterwards, there were men and women prepared and able to recognise him for what he was.

Our waiting for Christ to enter our lives can be merely passive. We may not be sure just what we are looking for. Or we can wait expectantly like children at the front gate waiting for their father to come home from work, and who know him as soon as he comes in sight.

Christ himself tells us to wait alertly like a householder who thinks a burglar is coming to break into his house. Our waiting is not just for killing time. During it, through prayer and reflection, and through our neighbour, we can come to know who it is that we are waiting for.

Christ comes to us in many different ways, some of them unexpected. We do not know the day or the hour of his coming, but while we wait we can prepare ourselves so that we recognise him at once whenever and wherever he comes into our lives.

For people who lived through the war, the words 'delayed action' have a sinister ring. They remind us of bombs which went off only some time after hitting the ground. They used to saw away at taut nerves, because nobody was sure whether or not they would explode, and when.

Delayed action waiting can also be hard on the nerves. The ship-wrecked sailor who watches a plane circling overhead, flying lower, and then turning away, hopes it has seen him, but is left waiting anxiously in case it has not. The patient in a doctor's waiting room is often left to wait, after the receptionist has taken down his name, and begins to wonder whether he has been forgotten.

The prisoner who knows that new evidence has established his innocence has to wait while the processes of law are completed. Often it seems that nothing is happening, although in fact a great deal is going on.

St John the Baptist was in this position. He had identified Jesus Christ as the Lamb of God. He knew that salvation was at hand. Yet he himself was imprisoned by Herod, and he was left languishing while the only one who could save him seemed to have forgotten all about him.

Eventually he sent two of his disciples to ask: "Are you the One who is to come, or should we look for someone else?" It was understandable impatience. There was Christ, working wonders for others, and leaving his own prophet neglected and suffering.

Yet Christ had not forgotten him, and later he was to pay John the compliment of saying that of all the children born of women a greater than John had never been seen.

In our lives, too, we can become similarly impatient and fretful. Christ has come, we believe, but it seems to make no difference to us. Other people seem favoured by God, other people succeed in great undertakings, but we ourselves languish in prison waiting for a sign, a grace, a deliverance which never comes.

It seems unfair. After we have made our act of faith in Christ, we feel we deserve to experience a direct and unambiguous display of God's power in our lives. But all he asks of us is to wait.

Like the Church itself, to which we belong, we have to wait, not knowing the day or the hour when Christ will come to complete the Kingdom which he has inaugurated.

Meanwhile we still have a part to play. Like John the Baptist we are expected to testify to the truth, in faith and humility, without looking for any immediate reward. We are asked to rejoice in the favours God does for others, and the dramatic works of others which build up the Kingdom of God on earth.

Meanwhile many are called to languish in prison, keeping their faith, hope and love alive, against all the odds. They are the Church's silent service. They include all the sick and suffering, who have nothing to offer but their own pain and neglect.

But God's action is only delayed. At the end of their patient waiting, through the faith they have kept alive, when Christ comes at the end of time, they too will be revealed as the greatest of all those born of women.

There is a great difference between just waiting and waiting in hope. Waiting which has no point to it is a deadly experience. But waiting in the positive expectation of some joyful gift or event has an undertone of excitement.

Christian waiting is of the second kind. The Christian waits as the Church waits, sustained by the hope reserved for him in heaven, the hope by which, St Paul tells us, we are saved.

Hope is a vital, perhaps the most vital, ingredient of human life. The hopeless man is a dead man. The man who has something to live for is the best equipped to deal with hardships, put up with disappointments, survive the keenest trials.

So during the war it was often remarked that in times of crisis, for instance when seamen had to drift for days on the open sea waiting for rescue, or when men and women had to endure unspeakable suffering in concentration camps, those survived best who were buoyed up by the kind of faith which is indistinguishable from hope.

The Christian is filled with hope. He waits to see. He waits for the fulfilment of his own humanity, the full flowering of his personality, in a further stage of existence.

He waits for the day when he will be reunited with all those he has loved on earth, without fear or threat of further separation.

He waits to see, face to face, the God who is the source of all that is good, attractive and lovable in this world. He awaits the day of the Lord, who will come with power to enlighten the eyes of his servants.

But his hope is not fatalism. Because he is full of hope the Christian is not embittered or defeated by the sadness and suffering of this world, nor merely resigned to it. He bends to the task of subduing the earth and setting human society to rights, knowing that this is what God asks of him during his time of waiting.

He knows that his own quiet efforts to transfigure the earth by the power of love will hasten the day when the Lord comes, and God will be all in all. But while he waits and works, the words of the Lord are always in his mind: I am the Resurrection and the Life; he who believes in me will never die.

THE RETURN OF MYSTERY

For a few days this summer we had two friends, both opera singers, staying with us. One evening they played recordings of their recent performances, she singing Isolde, he singing Simon Boccanegra. We sat or sprawled in the still, darkened garden, where not a leaf stirred and not a sound carried from the village or the surrounding fields and woods. Overhead myriads of stars twinkled brilliantly. And out of the house into the quiet night, where we each sat in our own cocoon of silence, poured this thrilling music—the solitary human voice climbing and descending the dense slow waves of the orchestra.

It was a moment of great mystery, indeed of many mysteries. Hard, first of all, to connect the two shadowy figures in jeans and tee-shirts sitting among us with those two tremendous voices throbbing majestically upon the night air. Hard, indeed, to believe that any human voice could utter such sounds, or any human frame contain such emotions, or that any human mind could in the first place conceive them and find such a language to express them. Hard also to register what each of us in our solitariness was taking in or what meaning each of us found in what we were hearing. Then round about us the mystery of the unheard teeming life of flower and tree and shrub, of animal and insect, above and below the ground, and the minute slippages and reactions of the very soil which gave them home and nurture. And finally, overhead, the canopy of stars: stars upon stars, galaxies upon galaxies, stretching out beyond the limits of comprehension, probed now to the edge of the universe by radio-telescopes and yielding up a million secrets to insistent, inquisitive man, yet still imposing the ultimate, tantalising question—Why? and Whence?

Everyone, I suspect, knows such moments. And they are, I also suspect, the fundamental experience which makes us feel sold short by mechanistic explanations of the universe and man's condition. The more "facts" we know, the more the whole seems greater than the parts. The more causes and effects are identified, the more the most vivid experience of being human seems left out of account. And the more the microscope and telescope reveal of the simple laws which underpin all life, the more the central mystery of the why and wherefore clamours for an answer. The cold rational universe we have been offered during the age of science, its minutest details docketed and documented, and its reduction of man to one outgrowth among many of the chemistry, physics and biology, seems to exclude all that is most intense, thrilling, moving and perplexing in human experience. Our dreams, our ideals, our conscience, our inspirations, our responsibilities. What light does this multitude of facts shed upon love, courage or self-sacrifice? What light does it shed, for example, upon the action of the British soldier who threw himself at Arnhem on a hand-grenade to save the life of a Dutch mother and child? Or upon the passions and denial of passions that are the stuff of mankind's literature? Or the sense of moral obligation to a Supreme Being on which Newman set such store? Or on Auschwitz or the Gulag?

The conception of a closed, entirely rational and wholly material universe has deeply influenced agnostic intellectual thought in the West, and even some modern theologians—ironically, for physicists themselves seem to be backing away from it as a result of what is sometimes called the new physics. Some years ago in his book *The Tao of Physics* Fritjof Capra noted this development and drew remarkable parallels between the most recent attempts to describe the properties and interactions of the subatomic particles of which all matter is made, and the descriptions of the inner nature of the world to be found among the mystics, the easterns especially. "Modern physics" he says, "leads us to a view of the world which is very similar to the views held by mystics in all ages and traditions", but this time "not only based on intuition but also on experiments of great precision and sophistication, and on a rigorous and consistent mathematical formulation". Very briefly this thesis, which reverses the western scientific assumption that the material universe has extended its empire at the expense of what has traditionally been called the "spirit", argues that the essential nature of our universe is not material but spiritual, that the closer we get to the heart of reality the more we encounter the paradoxical and the inexplicable, and that the truest vision of the universe leads out of science and indeed beyond rational thought and language.

One must not claim too much too hurriedly. But it will be odd indeed if out of science itself is reborn a fresh confidence in those intimations of mystery, those hints of the numinous which have so long been derided as superstition or wish-fulfilment or cowardly escapism, but which in truth sustain all religion.

THE LAST ENEMY

It is over a hundred years since we entered the age of the photograph. How it brings home the fact of death! Here is an ambulance-driver in the Crimea, bearded, huddled in his greatcoat, his cap awry, peering out resentfully at the strange new machine whose products he may never have seen. Despite his experience of life, so different from ours, and the sights he saw which have passed away, he is plainly one of us, and it seems for a moment possible to reach through the page and shake his hand. But he is dead. Here is a troopship, soldiers crowding the decks, singing lustily as it moves out into Southampton Water. All dead. Here is the Court of the Tsar, there a tennis party on the lawn of an English vicarage, and there a class of ragged children in a north-country town, and there a jam of carriages and drays in Piccadilly, and there a milling crowd of straw-hatted young men and long-skirted girls celebrating the Relief of Mafeking. Dead, all of them dead. No painted portrait brings home, as does the photograph, the fleshly reality of people in the past, who lived like us and are dead.

It is the scale of death which overwhelms almost as much as death itself. There are four billion people alive today, and all will die. Daily they pour through the gates of death, thousands upon thousands and millions upon millions. And yet, as we know, each death is negotiated and suffered as a particular death, and each sends out a few quiet ripples among relatives and friends before the dust of oblivion settles over it. On the one side, death is as common as salt, and there could be a kind of comfort in such a commonplace. On the other, no death is like my death, and however each of us may try to deceive himself like a soldier on the battlefield, that he at least will slip past death unnoticed, all know that they must square up to it. Sometimes death strikes like lightning. Sometimes, death moves inexorably towards us, picking off every friend and acquaintance, and infiltrating each of the senses, before the final assault. The certainty of death, and its particularity, have been the preacher's stock in trade since man began. Not less so since the advent of Christianity. *Nous mourons tous, et nous mourons tous les jours,* in Bossuet's sombre words. Life is so short. Death is certain. Let us use these years of dying to make a good death.

Make a good death. Once it seemed to be so simple. The Christian formula was so clear: keep the commandments, observe the Church's laws, pray daily, be faithful to the sacraments, and death would hold no fears. At the end the priest would come, absolve and anoint the dying in the bosom of his family, and after receiving the body of the Lord as food for his journey, the Christian would quietly, and almost triumphantly, breathe his last. No terror there. In the words of the Indian writer: 'Death was the extinguishing of a lamp, because the dawn had come'. Or as the Mass for the Dead has it, 'Life is changed, not taken away'. If Christian mourners mourned, they did so for themselves, not for the departed, entered at last into the light and bliss he was born for.

It is a pleasant picture, and there are deaths which almost uncannily follow that prescription. But I think it true to say that more and more Christians find that the classic prescription neither meets the problems of death which they confront, nor the realities of modern life as it is lived. Some of these problems are not peculiar to Christians. They are implicit in the paradoxes of death itself. The fact of death can be a spur: time is short, so that activity, experience, achievement, must be hurriedly packed in. At the same time death seems to make a nonsense of all endeavour and all achievement, as it wipes out love, suffering, art, thought, constructions and relationships, leaving only a scatter of artefacts and a handful of tales as a heritage to succeeding generations.

Again, death seems a natural process in the sense that all things die, man among them; yet there is a strong natural instinct to fight off death, delay it as long as possible, avoid it if we can. We wish to go gently into that good night, yet rage against the dying of the light. Thus the doctor, in the forefront of a whole industry which wrestles tirelessly with death, feels cheated when his efforts fail. Similarly, society protects its citizens with a thick hedge of laws to reduce the danger of death, and feels outraged when a mother's thoughtlessness or bad luck causes—as we think—unnecessary death. Almost all humdrum activity—labouring, shopping, cooking, eating, resting, cleaning, recreating—is part of an endless war against death. Health farms, cosmetics, slimming and dieting, are attempts to cheat or camouflage the signs and effects of mortality. Men know they will die, yet live as if they will not. They know they will die, yet keep the thought of death stubbornly at bay. They know they will die yet live in hope of discovering a last-minute antidote to death.

That is not the end of the paradoxes. In the here and now anything seems more real than death; at the moment of dying death seems more real than anything. Death is the shadow falling upon every human activity; and yet, as Jung observed, it is also the condiment that adds piquancy to every human activity. The element of risk, the spice of danger, is stirred into every human activity. Just as the moutaineer would find no satisfaction in his sport if he did not know he was pitting himself against death, so every act of faith, love, hope, every decision, every adventure, throughout the course of life is charged with excitement because the certainty of death attends it. ' I shall not pass this way again'. No, and at any moment the way may be closed for good. Terrible though it is to think of death rendering human achievements null and void, without it every achievement in life would be tasteless.

Christians are not immune from these tensions. Indeed they may be even more susceptible. To the fear of death and the pain of dying, they may add fear of everlasting hell. To the gamble implicit in every human act, they add the gamble on salvation, hope of reward and fear of punishments beyond imagining. Every decision is fraught with consequence not simply in the framework of this short life, but in the framework of eternity. If the unbeliever has reason to rail against a life on earth which seems as short as a blast on a whistle, in which so much seems possible and so little can be achieved, the believer may rail against being asked to stake so much on heaven, before he has time even to settle down and feel at home on earth.

However that may be, under the old dispensation the Christian seemed to derive little comfort from his hope of paradise, at least judging from his outward behaviour. Despite all the talk of entering a better life, and all the consoling rhetoric, the average mourners at an average Catholic funeral exhibited the same inconsolable grief as their pagan neighbours. There was a sense of doom, as if it must be presumed that only a lucky few would edge into heaven, and the dear departed unlikely to be among them.

The truth is that for many Christians their beliefs did not help them to face death; indeed, they not infrequently added to their anxiety. It could not be assumed that Christians would die serenely and confidently, unbelievers in an agony of despair. The unbeliever might die peacefully, sufficiently convinced that he had had his moment, that he was falling asleep for the last time, and that all further consciousness would now cease. The Christian might equally well die in a state bordering panic, overwhelmed by a sense of guilt and a fear of damnation. Those powerful mission and retreat sermons, whose spirit was so marvellously caught in James Joyce's

Portrait of the Artist as a Young Man, evoking unbearable physical torments for ever and ever, could enter the bloodstream, and it was not everyone who managed to overcome them with a truer sense of divine mercy. It is not difficult to see why. The rhetoric of mercy and eternal blessedness, the description of paradise, were altogether more pallid and more speculative than the heightened descriptions of pains whose earthly reality was already all too familiar. It was, and is, easier to describe a convincing hell than a convincing heaven. Similarly, large numbers of people find it easier to believe in their sins and frailties than their virtues, and a theology which spoke of salvation as the reward for keeping a bargain ('If you keep out of mortal sin, I will save you') could quickly undermine hope in people painfully conscious of their sinfulness. So, the rhetoric went one way—the certainty of life after death, the joys of paradise awaiting the faithful Christian—and the individual's feeling another. Far from rejoicing in the thought of being united with his risen Lord, many a Christian was as depressed by the physical signs of ageing, and the thought of approaching death, and as eager as any unbeliever, to put off the moment of death.

To this traditional predicament, changes in our modern mentality and way of life have added further difficulties which many Christians experience. For better or worse, when members of the Church could look up a detailed catalogue of sins with all their divisions and sub-divisions, at least they knew where they stood. Today there is a greater sense of moral ambiguity, greater emphasis on individual assessment of right and wrong, individual decision and individual responsibility. There is less stress on pre-packed right answers, more on ways of reaching a right answer and developing greater moral sensibility within the Christian community. This is to my mind a step in the right direction, but it leaves in tatters the old account-book system which brought assurance to many that they were 'right with God'. Positively, it can create a more Christian sense of salvation as God's free gift, a deeper and more loving and more trustful relationship with the redeeming Christ; negatively, it may sometimes lead to an ennervating sense of free-floating anxiety, heightened by the approach of death.

This particular revolution in the Christian approach to morality has been sparked by discontent with the gap between theory and experience. The old system simply did not ring true. But another reason for rejecting chessboard morality is the destructive, inhibiting effect it had on so many Christians of a nervous disposition. Far too many reduced the Christian life to keeping out of hot water. In order to do nothing wrong, they did nothing at all. They virtually sailed from cradle to grave with hatches battened down, lying on their bunks, while the boat sailed on automatic pilot. There was no place for risk, decision or enterprise. They believed like the character in the Gospel that the Lord was a hard master, and the safest thing was to bury their talent so that it could be produced for inspection on his return. Against this desolating interpretation there has also been a strong reaction. Life has to be lived positively, risks must be taken, there is room for doubt and failure, for these are not the end of the world. Holding God in awe is right and proper, but not in the sense that it stifles human capacities, renders life sterile, and breeds a paralysing caution.

A third reaction against the view that because the fulfilment of life lies beyond the grave, this world is of no account. Growing Christian involvement in political, social and economic matters, derives from the theological understanding that the building of the kingdom starts here. The prospect of heaven, the inadequacies of human justice and human endeavour, do not justify opting out of earthly concerns and pursuing a totally private, individualistic cultivation of the soul. Equally, increased understanding of salvation as effected for and in and through the Christian community—'Look not upon my sins but the faith of your Church'—steers the contemporary Christian in the same direction. The kingdom is among us, and we must play our part within it here and now. Keeping the thought of heaven in mind is one thing; but for the Christian to fix his eyes on the sunlit uplands that lie ahead, while ignoring the afflictions and distress all about him, is quite another. If the Christian is truly to adore 'in Him, and with Him, and through Him', it must in and with and through the people who are Christ's body.

At least two other shifts in sensibility are worth remarking. First a disinclination to take seriously the more picturesque and bloodthirsty descriptions of hellfire. This on two counts: one, that God cannot be more ruthless than his creatures, few of whom would wish to condemn even the worst of their fellows to everlasting torment; secondly, the—literal—pains Christ has gone to in order to bring home the loving, merciful and forgiving nature of his Father, far transcending the mercy and forgiveness shown by men. Though it is true that judged from the outside the deliberate malice and cruelty of human beings can be appalling (think only of the concentration camps), in normal human judgment there is a gross disproportion between the muddled confusion of conventional sin, and the rhadamanthine judgment passed on it by the wrathful God of hellfire preachers. It is possible to believe that in theory a person may grow such a carapace of selfishness and self-absorption that not even the love of God can touch his heart, but very difficult to believe that it happens often. The assumption must be that if there is a real choice at the moment of death between God and self, not the rather artificial choice in everyday life between a God glimpsed through a glass darkly and some object or advantage which may or may not be good but is most certainly there, the choice will fall on God. And nothing short of a real choice seems to square with God's justice.

Finally, the romantic picture of Christian death is badly blotched by the conventions of modern society, at least in urban, industrialised countries. We no longer live in villages or close-knit parishes where relatives and friends gather spontaneously round those who are sick unto death. People die in hospitals, or suddenly in accidents, or alone in their bed-sitters. Outside religious houses, only a lucky few are likely to die supported and comforted with their family praying at the bedside. It can and does happen, and such a classical Christian death is very moving. Only a few weeks ago I was one of a small gathering round the bedside of a priest uncle who was dying. It was a Sunday morning, with sunshine flooding the room. Mass had just finished, sung to music he himself had composed. As we said the prayers for the dying and recited the rosary—he died during the mystery of the resurrection—I was never more conscious of the need and the power of prayer; it seemed palpably to lift him through the final pains of dying and over the frontier of death. And from the moment of his death all of us were filled with a sense of exhilaration—the word is not too strong—which continued to fill the house. It was a perfect end to a marvellously rich life. But such occasions are rare, and the 'unprovided death' against which the Church bids us pray is, for most people, far more likely. For great numbers of people death comes at the end of a long purgatorial wait of years spent alone or among strangers; and though there may be priest and sacraments when the time comes, there is no provision of prayers and familiar presences to share the burden of dying.

So much for the problem. What can be done? Clearly there is a need to distinguish carefully between the Christian community's task of assisting its members to face and adjust to the experience of death, and its communication of belief in the resurrected life promised to his followers by Christ and guaranteed by his own rising from the dead. The two have frequently been confused in Christian preaching and in the minds of believers. But as I have already suggested, belief in the life to come does not necessarily make the business of dying easier, and those who do not believe may die contentedly. It is not belief in the resurrected life as such, but the whole context of our life of faith and our understanding of the bond between God and man, which affects the Christian's attitude to death. In short, the Church's task is far wider than simply preaching the certainty of everlasting life. Making a good death is the end of a long process of psychological adjustment, and there is a great deal in Christian experience and teaching which can help that process.

Adjusting to death. Believer and unbeliever alike have to face the fact of death, and come to terms with their sense of revulsion. It is everyman's experience. 'I will die. When, where, how? I do not wish to die. I fear to die.' However deliberately that knowledge is pushed to the back of the mind, however determinedly a person concentrates on whatever seems to put back the prospect of death and make the present golden—sex, art, work, or to create an illusion of permanence—a comfortable home, financial security, the best possible medical care, and so forth—always the certainty of death is drumming quietly away like the engines in the bowels of a ship. To live with that certainty is the greatest demand made upon man. Some react by throwing themselves into a life of feverish self-indulgence—'Gather your roses while ye may'. Others sink into a state of apathy—'Why bother?' Others escape into various kinds of illusion, familiar to the psychiatrist. Neurosis and schizophrenia are both, at bottom, ways of repressing the certainty of death.

The Christian community's purpose must be to help people live positively and realistically between the poles of panic and apathy. That means stressing the value of all human activities as well as the dignity and value of every individual regardless of the accidentals—power, wealth, status, etc.—by which society judges a life to be 'successful'. It means bringing out in a way that carries conviction the lovableness of all human beings in the eyes of God. It means rooting in the benignity of God, revealed through Christ, the fact that the universe is ultimately friendly. And it means enabling people, through experiencing acceptance within the Christian community, to realise that their imperfect best is 'good enough', even if it falls short of their own and the community's ideals. The Christian dies most easily who has grown into a true conviction that God loves and loves him, and in the healing presence of that love has accepted himself truthfully with all his strengths and his structural weaknesses, all his failings and follies, all his genuine achievements, however minor. And that conviction, it need hardly be said, normally grows through the loving sympathy and acceptance of other human beings, meditating the divine love which informs all human love. To die without regrets, truthfully, without illusions about one's vices and virtues, accepting and accepted: this is the ideal. And it comes out of a deepening understanding and broadening vision of God's dealings with us, once again mediated through the Christian community as it has actually been experienced, rather than pious romantic notions about death, or even intellectual adherence to the doctrine of the resurrection. Death will normally be of a piece with life, and those come to terms with death who have gradually come to terms with life. If a person's understanding of what is expected of a Christian during life is wrong, then his understanding of what is expected at death will be wrong also. If a person embarks upon death filled with romantic pictures of ethereal saints filled with virtues and graces, looking back on an unblemished life, and triumphantly assured of entering paradise on merit, something has gone seriously wrong in their previous comprehension of their faith. Christian life and teaching should strip away illusions, not add to them.

Christian teaching on detachment and self-sacrifice plainly helps towards making a good death. Those especially who have lived heartily, revelled in the joys and riches each has to offer, and been fortunate in those they have loved and been loved by, will find it hard to leave behind all that is so dear. To break with a beloved home, wife, children, satisfying work, a whole range of pleasures and satisfactions to pass into the unknown: that is very hard. Again the knack cannot be acquired at a stroke. The balancing trick which enables us to live enthusiastically in the present, love deeply and create with conviction, while at the same time recognising that everything is contingent and provisional, is not acquired in a day. The secret is to love without wishing to possess, to relish what other human beings and the earth itself offer us as gifts, without becoming dependent on them or feeding ravenously on them to support our self-esteem. A habit of penance of self-sacrifice which allows self to develop through the service of others keeps the raging Ego in check, cultivates a good-humoured acceptance of our own limitations, and enables us to value all creatures while keeping everything in proportion. When we have learned to give up gracefully the small, dear things of life, there is a good chance that we will gracefully surrender life itself. There are, heaven knows, opportunities enough in the course of living. 'Each time we part I die a little', as the old song says. Every parting is a training exercise for death, a little death, whether it is parting with a comfortable old sweater, a house that has grown fond and familiar, a job in which one has been happy, or a beloved wife or husband.

The other key to making a good death is, I believe, a steady growth in honesty with oneself accompanied by deepening appreciation of God's loving nature. The two go together. The humbug we practise on ourselves can so often be traced to a hidden fear that we serve a severe God who must at all costs be placated. The temptation then is to draw down blinds on the shoddier elements in our personality, camouflage or excuse what is mean and vicious, the waste and the failures, to trick ourselves and, so we may hope, God himself. But God cannot be tricked, and neither can we. Only when we have learned complete confidence in God's unfailing love, and total acceptance of every human being, warts and all, are we likely to face ourselves with ruthless honesty and accept tranquilly the dark side of our own nature. And the Cross is the window through which we come finally to understand the quality of divine love, and through which we find the strength to face the truth about ourselves without panic or despair. Only then, too, that we cease to bargain with God and know in our hearts that salvation is truly a gift offered to all willing to receive it.

Once again I return to the Christian community as a school for dying well. It is there that it should be possible to experience the freedom to be honest, and a love without qualifications or conditions: love neither sentimental nor sickly, but robust and sympathetic, love that supports and accepts people as they are. If the community acts as a public prosecutor, judge and jury, the God its members come to know will be a caricature. Likewise if it demands service, revels in its power, belittles the individual, scorns where it is asked only to forgive. If it acts so, it will add its own stings to the pain of death, and death will truly be the last enemy. But if through it, the true God has been glimpsed, however darkly, death will hold no fears but be welcomed as a friend.

I have said nothing, deliberately, about belief in life after death and its bearing upon the Christian's attitude to death. Plainly, those who believe that death is a terminus, and those who truly believe it to be a gateway opening onto a further stage of existence will approach death very differently; to quote Hopkins, 'God, lover of souls, swaying considerate scales, complete thy creature dear O where it fails'. The belief that God offers man eternal blessedness, and that Christ has opened the way to it, is of course the mainspring of Christian life. The Christian community's task is to proclaim that belief and the evidence for it, and to create conditions in which the individual can steadily grow more confident of it.

All I would say is that often enough popular preaching is an obstacle to this process by which the individual makes the common belief his own. Perhaps detailed descriptions of the joys of heaven are less common than they used to be, but still they occur; and very disagreeable they usually are. And endless hippie rally on the Isle of Wight is not everyone's dream of paradise, nor a kind of football chant, even addressed to the Almighty, lasting for all eternity. Even talk of banquets and wedding feasts does not enthuse every breast. Better perhaps to talk strictly in pauline terms of continuity between the personality here below, like the seed in the ground, and its ultimate fulfilment, like the tree or the flower which eventually appears above ground; or the pleasures of this world as a foretaste of that which eye hath not seen nor ear heard that God has prepared for those who love him. If Christians show few signs of eagerly running to paradise, it may be because the paradise they hear described is not a place to which any reasonable person would wish to go.

I remember finally a man who had come to terms with death, learned confidence in a loving God, and believed in and looked forward to paradise. He was an old French Jesuit. When his last moments had come, a few scholastics were asked to pray by his bedside. As they stood there, suitably grave and recollected, the old man opened one eye and said in a weak voice, 'Open the drawer at the foot of the cupboard'. One of them did so and found a bottle of champagne and some glasses. 'Fill up your glasses' the old man said. One of the scholastics did as he was told and they stood for a moment wondering what to say next. The old man opened up the other eye and said rather gruffly, 'What about me?' So they gave him a glass. Then he said, 'I've lived a very happy life. I'd like you to drink with me to a happy death'. They drank the toast, and five minutes later he died. A good death: but then he had spent his life learning to love his enemies.

DATE DUE

HIGHSMITH   # 45220